Why WORRY *When* GOD...

SCRIPTURAL THERAPY FOR ANXIETY

CARL H. MONTGOMERY, II

Unless otherwise indicated, Scripture quotations are from the King James Version of the Bible (KJV). MONT denotes personal translation by author. Take note that the name satan and related names are not capitalized. We choose not to acknowledge him, even to the point of violating grammatical rules.

CHARIS HOUSE PRESS
Publishers
a division of
GRACE OF GOD MINISTRIES, INC.
13 East 20th Street
Baltimore, Maryland 21218

Library of Congress Control Number: 00-091448

Montgomery, II., Carl H.
Why Worry When God: Scriptural Therapy for Anxiety / Carl H. Montgomery, II

Includes bibliographical references.
ISBN 0-9678976-0-2
1. Spirituality--Religious aspects--Christianity. 2. Self Help--Therapy 3. Success in life--Psychological aspects. I. Title.

Printed in the U.S.A.

Cover design by Bernice Twum-Barimah

Dedicated

To my wife, Sheila and Gennele, my daughter, the most unique combination of love, support, and encouragement. "*Sheila, this started because of you. You wanted me to complete this effort and you prayed me through. Now may this book be a symbol of the enormous magnitude of your love and inspiration. I love you both!*"

To the sainted Mother Geneva Bruce-Montgomery, whose greatest achievement in life was the cultivation of righteous seeds and fruit that would remain.

"*Your memory is truly blessed.*"

CONTENTS

Acknowledgements

An effort such as this would not be possible were it not due to the input of others who became as enthusiastic about this project as I; not to mention those who have affected me by the influence of their lives.

To my Greater Grace Church family for your love and encouragement. The principles here have been practiced by you and you have challenged me to share them with others.

Thanks to my staff; Bernice Twum-Barimah, whose technical skills and artistry makes her a perfectionist worth knowing; and to DeAnne Wade, for your loyal and faithful assistance on this and everything you put your hands to do.

Thank you to Tabitha Jones, for your inspiration and proficient assistance. You dared to believe!

Special thanks to my joy, my daughter, Gennele, for her professional support. You sharpen my iron.

Thanks to Lady 'De', Delicia Garnes, for your attention to my project in the middle of your professional pursuits.

Thank you to my covenant brother, mentor and apostolic covering, The Most Reverent J. Delano Ellis, II, for your fatherly faith and confidence in me as a spiritual leader in the Lord's Church. Mostly, thanks for your fearlessness and loyal friendship.

To the sainted memory of Bishop Winfield and Mother Genevieve Showell for your years of guidance and personal tutelage which has brought us here! Gone but not forgotten.

PREFACE

WHO WOULD have thought that this book would have evolved from a Sunday morning sermon? Certainly not I! The bishop had been preparing us for a different book, which was to be his first. Then came the article "Managing Worry: Your Passport to Peace" which was published in the Fall/Winter 1999 issue of the church's newsletter, *The Olive Branch.* The requests began to pour in, "You should publish a part two of that article... I never considered worry in that light..." That's how it all started.

Indeed, what a new light it has provided! This book consists of a liberating message, clearly defined explanations, and practical candor. *Why Worry When God* is an evolution of rhema. The understanding on this subject is reflective of the illuminated use of Scripture and the Light of the Word used by the author in his personal exodus from a dark wilderness.

We challenged the title, at first, until we read the manuscript. In every chapter God is magnified. Everything He is exalted over disappears as His awesome presence dispels all doubts, worries and fears. Not realizing how convenient worry had become for me I have finally learned just how useless its existence is. This book will empower you to take charge of your thoughts, and bring them captive to the Holy Spirit's peaceful confidence. Enjoy it! I certainly have!

Yeve Gennele Montgomery
Managing Editor, *The Olive Branch*

INTRODUCTION

AT FIRST GLANCE the title of this book may appear to be incomplete. However, it should simply be considered an open-ended question and for good reason. While most titles make a statement, however, this one allows the reader to involve himself in the process of discovery. By so doing each individual is afforded the opportunity to fully develop and complete the title question for himself, thereby affirming a personal statement of confidence and trust. It is only through one's experience, with a knowledge of God and how He makes Himself known in impossible situations, that an individual is enabled to emphatically affirm His divine ability with any degree of conviction.

Why Worry, When God cares, knows what's best, is in control and has your best interest at heart? You see no one knows how best to finish this sentence for *you*. Whether you are a non-worrier, occasional worrier or a worrywart you will be compelled to reach your own conclusion to this question while prayerfully walking through this literary endeavor.

In essence, this book is the culmination of years of experience encompassing various trials and errors. Although varying in importance from one episode to another each experience has found a common relationship with worry or at least have had some remote connection. This endeavor is not only a personal retrospective journey but it too encompasses collective counseling experience which also reveals a common thread of worry in most regretful judgement. The issue of worry has paralyzed dreams, halted visions, exasperated efforts and reduced determination to futile possibilities. This menace must be stopped and its impact eliminated.

Through this effort you will be compelled to reflect upon and re-evaluate past issues once you see the devastating contribution worry has made towards circumstances in your life. You will experience Scripture, however familiar, from a new perspective when viewed in light of worry. Ultimately, you will reassess your misconceptions about this emotional trait and acknowledge its detrimental characteristics.

My prayer is that by the time you finish this book you will conclude with a new affirmation derived from a renewed faith gleaned from these pages. Finally, my prayer is that through the Holy Spirit you will conquer fears, complete tasks, initiate visions, perfect projects and perform all that is within you. As Samuel said to Saul, ***"Do as occasion serves you!"*** (*ref.* I Samuel 10:7) It is true that the greatest natural resources in the earth are not in the diamond mines of Africa nor in the oil wells of all of OPEC combined. Instead to the surprise of many, it is within the desolate, dejected and dismal graveyards throughout the world. It is there that the earth is permeated with unrealized potentials, undeveloped talents, dreams unfulfilled and hopes which are forever deferred.

Furthermore, it must be said that too often something as subtle as worry and as drastic as fear is the secret culprit ensuring that the resources of the graveyard are never depleted. There comes a time when you must get a grasp on what God has promised to His people, know what He thinks of you, and live when others say die! You really have not lived until you have weathered the storms of adversity only to rise above the earthly elements designed to bury you. I've found this one fact to be most important when facing your promised destiny; that you can't merely accommodate those who want you to die simply because your existence troubles them. You must live even when *you* don't feel it. You must survive and thrive even in the face of oppositions which appear to prevail. If you fail to approach life with this type of stamina you too will take your visions and dreams to the grave and leave this world deprived of your many contributions.

For this reason you will also find in this book the liberal utilization of Scripture. It is my desire to utilize a scripturally-therapeutic approach to the treatment of the soulish ills of many Christian believers. By prescribing moderate yet balanced dosages of scriptural answers for practical living the believer will better understand the guidance and work of the Holy Spirit and the benefits derived from submission to divine authority. This approach is not to the exclusion of inter-disciplinary treatments of persons experiencing severe or deep-rooted problems. However, it is by all means, an answer for those believers who wish to experience balanced, abundant living void of unnecessary anxiety. Hence, these passages are provided throughout the various chapters as life-support verses, which I discovered or became personally reacquainted with while in the valley of death.

1

A COMMON FOE

". . . Most don't even recognize that worry isn't something one has to become accustomed to nor resolve to live with throughout one's life . . . it should be perceived at worst as a repulsive enemy and a common foe at best."

AT THE ONSET of this undertaking, I was surprised to learn how many people thought it unnecessary to discuss, let alone write about the topic of worry. I found many that admitted they do worry from time to time, but their common belief, as so often stated was, "Everybody worries!" Some even confessed, "It's no big deal, it's just a part of life!" The current age in which we live is described as "the age of anxiety." Anxiety for our high-tech era, however, is considered a by-product of day-to-day life. This widespread acceptance of worry and anxiety has made it the most common of all unpleasant emotional states.

However, it's this common acceptance of worry that concerned me and caused me to explore the subject. While many admit they do worry they also had to confess that worry had in fact, been directly linked to or had an effect upon their desires, aspirations and dreams. It was this closer examination of anxiety that made me realize worry is a prevalent and familiar foe that influences the lives of all human beings. It is so common and appears to come so naturally that an inordinate number of individuals have mastered how to live with it. Moreover, most don't even recognize that worry isn't something one has to become accustomed to nor resolve to live with throughout one's life. In fact, at worst, it should be perceived as a repulsive enemy and a common foe at best. The truth is, for most, the effects of their anxiety are negative no matter how shrewd in characteristics they may be. While conceptualizing the strategy for this subject I discovered some things that will hopefully place worry where it belongs and open for us a whole new world of divine dependence, peaceful repose, and a confidence which is immovable.

In order for us to explore the subject we must arrive at a practical definition of the word "worry". I learned that "...worry is typically an uncomfortable emotional state that almost everyone experiences. Similar to most feeling states, worry can be placed on a continuum from chronic and intrusive to mild and constructive."[1] In other words, some may utilize worry in some minimal or purposeful way to achieve a task or goal. But worry, rating anywhere from a moderate to extreme level, can also be so severe in its effect that it can be associated with sickness, disease and even death. Consequently, "worry is a process rather than an event or state of being."[2]

Worries are generally birthed when there is either an external or internal threat which appears to have an impact on one's future. When one hears a negative report, or diagnosis for example, that individual may be troubled by what he's heard in relation to how it will affect his future and then begin to worry. However, many have managed not to sweat the small stuff.

We Worry About Our Worries

THE LARGER NUMBER of individuals have a tendency to attribute far too much attention to objects of worry. In fact, the object of true concern often goes unattended while we worry about our worries. Take for example an individual who has been thrust into the role of caretaker for a suddenly and chronically ill significant other. If not careful this caretaker can become so consumed with the impending plight and the day-to-day issues surrounding the illness that he or she may neglect opportunities for quality time with his sick loved-one. Instead he should seize the precious moments they have together.

When we understand worry in this light we can see why God became so wroth with Israel in their response to the negative report brought back by the ten spies. They became so consumed with the worries surrounding the bad news they heard that they immediately forgot who they were and, more importantly, *whose* they were. They forgot God. (*ref.* Numbers 13, Deuteronomy 1:19-46) Eventually the Israelites realized the enormous transgression they had committed by vexing God with their distrust and rebellion. Israel attempted to prove their faith in God by making an effort to fight the very enemy they so feared. What a big mistake! God was not impressed! You see, God had already warned them against any confrontation with the enemy because He would not be with them in the fight! Because they'd already envisioned themselves as grasshoppers in comparison to their enemy, Israel had begun to worry that they would not be victorious. Accordingly, God granted them the *visual manifestation* of *their* fears instead of *His* benevolent-victory.

Ultimately in life, what you see is what you get! If you look at things through the eyes of defeat and failure then that's exactly what you will experience. If you can look at *impossible* situations and see *possibilities* then your *possibilities* will become *realities*.

Worry Can Keep Us Wandering in Circles

ISRAEL WORRIED NEEDLESSLY and it cost them their inheritance. They forfeited their blessing because of their unbelief and suspicion. What a tremendous lesson this is for us! This is the essence from which we expose the root of all doubt and unbelief. Isn't worry at the core of all our fears? Some would debate "which comes first, worry or fear?" However, I believe the greater point between fear and worry is not seeing the relationship as *linear* but *cyclical*. By viewing this relationship from a cyclical perspective we can become aware of its impact regardless of which appears to be more prevalent. Hence, worry can keep us wandering in circles between doubt and fear. Consequently, we can easily trace those apprehensions that once immobilized us from accomplishing some goal all the way back to common worry.

Considering the aforementioned plight of the Israelites Joshua and Caleb were the only two of that worry-prone generation who were allowed to go over to the place of promise, simply because they possessed *"another spirit."* While their counterpart spies incited worry and panic Joshua and Caleb stilled the people. They said, ***"Let us go up at once, and possess it; for we are well able to overcome it."*** (*ref.* Numbers 13:30) In essence, their response to the people was "*Why worry when God* has given us victory over the opposition." They may have also refrained, *"Why worry when* we are well able to possess what God has promised!" Whatever the verbal sentiment may have been it is clear that they maintained a worry-free spirit which produced a trust in God. Since worrying will produce doubt then not worrying will bring about trust. Of course this sort of equation applies to the child of God whose thoughts and confidence are not in this world but are in the Lord. But it is also the formula by which thousands of successful people, unbelievers included, have achieved their dreams and goals. This brings me to another point of consideration with reference to the scriptural passage above.

Worry can be transferred by words. The people of Israel did not see for themselves what God had promised, they were going on the fearful words of the spies. This was their big mistake. If they had trusted the Word of the Lord they would have simply prepared themselves to possess, not to investigate! Moses only sent the spies because the people requested it and God allowed Moses to grant them their request. Ultimately, God put them in a position to exercise faith, like Joshua and Caleb, that would have brought them the victory.

Having the opinions and expressed worries of others can induce a spirit of doubt that's hard from which to recover. Therefore, it's best not to analyze when God gives you a word. Simply accept the fact that He knows best and that He is in control of every facet which may affect His provisions.

Adam and Eve worried so intensely about what God said not to do that they missed out on all He told them they could do! They had a thousand to one chance of losing everything. What tremendous odds for divine provision! There was only one tree in the midst of thousands that they could not touch. With odds this great in their favor, worry over the one thing they could not have caused them to sin, lose the abundance of God's provisions and become expelled from paradise. They had a word from God and while they listened to the serpent analyzing the ramifications of what God meant they began to worry about what God was possibly keeping from them. When the serpent said, ***"Ye shall not surely die: For God doth know that the day ye eat thereof, then your eyes shall be opened, and ye shall be as gods, knowing good and evil."*** (*ref.* Genesis 3: 4-5) Their response should have been, "Why worry when God knows what's best!" Nonetheless, we can clearly see that in both illustrations there is a spirit manifested within worry which, if left to incubate and mature, will eventually produce for us a dangerous monster of unbelief and disobedience.

We Must View Worry As A Covert Spy

DEMONSTRATED CONFIDENCE and trust in God can be as uncomplicated as refusing to worry beyond His words. After all, isn't that what trusting is all about? I believe Joshua and Caleb had the answer to all of our everyday problems. That is, possessing an attitude that essentially says, "if God made us a promise and was faithful enough to bring us this close to witnessing it, then why can't He give it to us, regardless of the opposition we see?"

We hear messages and sermons about doubt and unbelief, but if we can overcome worry we will be on the road to dispelling the doubts and fears that impede our progress towards a faith that pleases God. And when we come to the realization of how utterly impossible it is to please God without faith we will readily examine every facet of our lives for overt and covert hindrances to our faith. Understanding this fact of faith we must view worry as a covert spy, which secretly delivers the wrong message to our minds and our spirits thereby affecting our faith. The chief aim of covert spy activity is to attempt co-inhabitancy, blending into the common fiber of society without being detected. And, as with most espionage activity, the spy gains its power and influence by living commonly with and among the things it wishes to affect.

Hence, the true enemy of the children of Israel was not the giants and occupants of the promised land, instead it was the familiar spies who brought back the report and who continued to reside among them as agents of fearful doubt. No matter how ordinary and familiar your source of worry may be it must always be seen for what it really is, *a common foe.*

Once you detect its presence in your life you must immediately call attention to its existence. This can be done by identifying thoughts which cause anxiety. Next, these thoughts must be evaluated based upon their positive or negative impact upon the source of the anxiety. Finally, everything within you must rally to dispel it with all the fury and fervor exhibited by Joshua and Caleb.

2

IT REALLY DOESN'T MATTER

"You may not be able to change how you came on the scene of life, but you can determine how your being will impact your time and the future of those who will follow you. Once you come to these kinds of conclusions, you will realize other non-essential issues really don't matter."

AS WE COMPREHEND worry from a biblical perspective, we quickly discover three primary factors associated with it. First, we learn that worry is immaterial, meaning it has no real substance. Why? Worry can't change anything. Generally we worry as though there is some characteristic within the act itself that will bring about a change in the things we're worrying about. The truth is, in the course of worrying, we are the only things that change. As we discovered from the passages in Numbers 13, Israel's worrying and doubt did in fact change things for them—it ultimately changed their divine destiny! Instead of having access to forty years of God's unfolding and manifested promises, they experienced the change derived from a wilderness death induced by compulsive and exhaustive wandering. In the final analysis, they too became contributors to that vast reservoir of natural resources buried in the earth. In the end, the wilderness became their graveyard of unfulfilled destinies, dreams and realities.

Worry Programs You for Mediocrity

ONE CAN ONLY IMAGINE what it must have been like for Israel to realize that they were at the entrance of what God promised, but could only wander around it, disoriented and oblivious to the blessings before them. In essence this was their death before their demise. Whenever hopes, visions and dreams die within the spirit of a man it's only a matter of time before the rest of that man is placed in the ground. Israel was just outside of Canaan but could not go in. Soon the flame of their desire to enter dwindled down to a flicker that was ultimately extinguished under the breath of God. They saw the promise but were incapable of possessing what they saw because their spirits were now programmed to wander about instead of claiming the promise. It's almost as if their fears, worries, and doubts became a computerized chip in their wills that deprogramed them from conquering and occupying to complacency and mediocrity. Once mediocrity sets in you lose the essence of vision. The opportunity is reduced to an expendable option. What a punishment! This was Israel's fate for worrying about the report they'd heard and not taking God at His word.

How many people have you encountered who appear to fit this description? When we see this trait manifested we call it a lack of drive or motivation, or simply not having any ambition. Could it not be that their worries, doubts and fears have blown an essential circuit within their spirits, which would otherwise spark their faith for action? By worrying we become anxious, nervous, perplexed, and the list goes on. This kind of data will short-circuit your spiritual, emotional and mental drive. However, trusting in God and His promises not only settles our spirits but also creates for us a confidence which has a long list of benefits, benefits which surpasses our own understanding. In short, while there are exceptions to the rule, it is safe to conclude that the greater percentages of achievers are nonworriers. Of course, there are nonworriers who are also slothful and lazy. The greater message, however, is if you are going to fulfill your destiny and purpose you must acquire a worry-free approach to life. Remember, worry is a friend to mediocrity.

In order to achieve one must be willing to take purposeful risk. Successful people, especially those who are in covenant with God, are not afraid to take the necessary risk to obtain the unseen. You see we walk by faith and not by sight. However, when doing so, one should exercise caution and concern. By all means, there should first be a *"counting of the cost."* (*ref.* Saint Luke 14:28) Hence, planning for success and achievement will reduce worries and increase faith. If one creates a business plan for example, it is not an indication of the lack of faith, but it, in fact, reveal the extent to which one is exercising his faith.

Problems occur everyday. They seem to be a part of life. Simply put, stuff happens. Worrying is not the way God wants His children to deal with their problems. Jesus poses a question to us in His Word by asking ***"Which of you by taking thought can add one cubit to His stature?"*** (*ref.* Saint Matthew 6:27) Another way of saying this is "After you've contemplated it, can you really do a thing about it?" This passage should serve as a tremendous boost to our self-esteem and an antidote to low self-concept.

As I communicate with people I am amazed at the things many people worry about, especially in the areas of one's person. Things such as looks, personality, accomplishments, acceptance, relationships, status or position. I once spoke with an individual who complained about how others perceived him. He rehearsed the comments of others and I could see that he was internalizing these views. Knowing much about this individual's talents, accomplishments and intelligence, I began to inquire about them. As we concluded discussing the positive things, I recommended when confronted with the negative remarks of others the next time, inform them of what good and positive things you *have* done and *are* doing. Make them face the fact that there may be some things about yourself you may never be able to change because they are out of your control, but there are things you are doing which have made changes in your life for the better. Tell them,"Either we talk about the positive things or nothing at all!"

You can't change your looks, but you can improve upon your *outlook*. You can't change your height but you can change your *horizon*. You may not be able to change how you came on the scene of life, but you can determine how your existence will impact your time here and the future of those who will follow you. Once you come to these kinds of conclusions you will realize other non-essential issues really don't matter. You have an opportunity to make your existence matter! When it is your time to die this world should have known you were here!

A Marked Difference Between Believers and Non-Believers

WE MUST MOVE beyond 'small stuff' into a realm of achievement. All worry, regardless of what it's associated with, must be abandoned. In Matthew 6:30, Jesus clearly establishes for us that worry is synonymous with doubt because Jesus indelibly brands those who *"take thought"* or worry as those *"of little faith."* This further establishes the contrast between believers and non-believers, and this contrast is more than just a spiritual one. It means that as believers our fields of concern, as compared to non-believers, are different. This is why Jesus said, ***"...For after all these things do the Gentiles seek..."*** (*ref.* vs. 32) He is substantiating the fact that the child of God should not be prone to worrying over the same situations that plague non-believers. We are told to ***"...seek ye first the kingdom of God, and His righteousness; and all these things shall be added unto you."*** (*ref.* vs. 33) This means that more than the basic necessities of life will be added to us. The *"all things"* stated in that passage actually means the sky is the limit to what you can have, accomplish, or be! And, this is not the same *'name it and claim it!'*

Therefore, we have an assurance that what we don't see or have will be added according to the will of God as we prioritize His righteous kingdom. We must learn to say, "I don't have it but it will be added." What a powerful challenge if only we would stop quoting it and instead order ourselves to live by it. For even the best of us this task is easier said then done. The first step to being on your way to achieving this goal (with the help of God and the practice of His Word) is to cease from anxiety. This is a process that will only come into fruition as we practice. And you know the old saying, "Practice makes perfect." This is more than just a saying it is actually biblical.

The Word of God says, ***"Learn to do well"*** (*ref.* Isaiah 1:17). It is admonishing us that good performance and excellence is not accidental, it is achieved through practice. Paul said, ***"Be ye imitators (followers) of me, even as I am of Christ."*** (*ref.* I Corinthians 11:1 ASV) He is not talking about lining up behind him as he walks! He is actually saying, *"imitate me as I imitate Christ"* or *"practice my behavior as I practice His example."* It is only through the process of holiness that we are perfected. It must be pursued and practiced. We must practice godly living by modifying the deeds of the flesh.

Confess Not to Worry

IN LIKE MANNER we must also practice how to exercise faith by diminishing our worries. Changing one's words is the best place to begin in changing one's behavior. How many times have you heard it said, "I have too much to worry about" or "I have bigger or better things to worry about?" That's just it—you don't have to worry about anything! Be concerned? Yes! Give consideration to issues? Without a doubt! Worry or fret? Absolutely not! For me, once I started changing my verbal expressions and resolved not to worry, I began to look for other ways of handling conflict and problem situations. I found myself saying audibly:

> *"I'm not going to worry about that! Now Lord, since you have instructed me not to worry I will walk in obedience since I also know that to worry is to dishonor You and Your presence in my life. Therefore, I need you to provide me with the answers and solutions or the direction needed to confront these issues and bring proper closure to these matters!"*

Although I am challenged in this area almost daily, due to the vision and the responsibility given to me, I am discovering God's grace for each day just as He gives new mercies. As He makes a way of escape He also provides answers of wisdom for those who would ask Him. Most importantly, He gives grace and peace while we wait.

3

DON'T BE IRRESPONSIBLE

"Don't fool yourself; it takes time to worry! Worry consumes time and time is valuable. The older one becomes, the sooner he realize he must become a better steward of his time."

AS WE COME face to face with the second aspect of worry we must allow ourselves the freedom to explore new concepts in examining anxiety. By doing this we will understand the second aspect of worry: Worry is actually irresponsible. A person who is considered responsible is viewed positively. The characteristics of a responsible person are synonymous with those of one who is serious, trustworthy, and reliable, as well as mature. When considering this fact I'm compelled to also add "one who is a good steward" to the list. A good steward is often considered a good manager or custodian of others' property. We may not readily consider this paradigm when considering mental activity or thought patterns, but the principles of stewardship can equally apply to our manner of thinking as well as to our behavior.

In stewardship, one can be a good or a poor administrator of his thoughts. What goes on in our minds is due largely in part to what we allow ourselves to concentrate on. Hence, our minds are the battlegrounds for many demonic attacks. If we surrender our thoughts to satan it won't be long before he will ultimately utilize our actions to achieve his plan for our destruction. Since our thoughts are associated with our deeds they too must categorically be accounted for through our physical actions. Paul instructs us to ***"Let this mind be in you which was also in Christ Jesus: Who... made Himself of no reputation and took upon Him the form of a servant... and being found in fashion as a man, He humbled Himself and became obedient unto death, even the death of the cross"*** (*ref.* Philippians 2: 5-8) .

Jesus Christ, the Son of God, who became the Son of man, exhibited for us the necessity of mental stewardship. The eventual victory Christ achieved at Calvary was begun when He surrendered Himself to an initial mind-set. It was His mind-set towards His mission, purpose, obligation and entrusted responsibility, which lead to His actions of obedience, focus of task, and achievement of assignment. This was no easy chore! Mostly because Jesus, who is God in the flesh, had to do something He had never done before as God: He had to *"learn"* obedience! As God, Christ knew everything there was to know, after all He created everything and ***"by Him all things consist"*** (*ref.* Colossians 1:17). Yet the one thing that would help Him accomplish the will of His Father had to be learned! Remember, He is God! Therefore, who else was there for Him to obey? But when God came in the likeness of sinful flesh to die for sin Christ Jesus was made to learn obedience and this was a lesson that could only be accomplished through submissive-suffering.

Now [if] Jesus Christ was very God and very man, as man

He could only experience genuine suffering where there was genuine struggle. There can only be a struggle when there is an alternative, challenge, or conflict. If one comes through the conflict, overcomes the challenges, and ignores the alternatives, it's because he have developed the mind-set to accomplish it.

The Mind Of Christ

IF THIS IS TRUE in the natural it is even more so in the spiritual sense. Jesus could not have obeyed God's will without first *a mind.* And this is evident in the events surrounding the wilderness temptations of Jesus by satan, as well as the challenges and struggles of Jesus in the Garden of Gethsemane. Christ's mind played an intricate part in His ability to bring about our eternal salvation. He resigned Himself to not seek His own well-being but to do the will of His Father no matter what the cost. His example admonishes us, those now saved by His grace, to also seek the mind of Christ, Who is ***"... the author of eternal salvation unto all them that obey Him..."*** (*ref.* Hebrews 5:9) As Christians, when we refer to the"'mind of Christ" we often make this term equivalent to *"the will of God".* His will is made known through the Word of God.

To seek the mind of Christ, however, is to ascertain something quite different: We are seeking to *think* as Christ would think when we are challenged in areas of struggles. Jesus came as our perfect example, but we will never achieve His example if we don't start with a particular mind-set, *His.* Hence, the mind of Christ is the pathway to God's will.

Today there is a popular expression revealed in the letters, "WWJD" which stand for the question "What Would Jesus Do?" It's not until we get the mind of Christ that we will know exactly what Jesus would do in any situation. Jesus' mind-set was to please and obey the Father and to complete

His assignments. Jesus sought these goals not for the purpose of seeking personal fame but to bring glory to His Father by revealing the Father's will. Paul, in his revelation of this truth, declared ***"With my mind I serve the law of God..."*** (*ref.* Romans 7:25) And this he got from beholding Christ's example, though he personally never followed Jesus while Christ was here in the flesh!

Consequently, because of Christ's determined mind-set not to waiver from His Father's assignment God rewarded Him for His obedience. God recognized that in order for Christ to complete the assignment given to Him He had to be an obedient Son. Therefore, God's exaltation of His Son is greatly and justly deserved. For God has ***"highly exalted Him and given Him a name which is above every name: that at the name of Jesus every knee should bow and every tongue should confess, that Jesus Christ is Lord to the glory of God the Father."*** (Philippians 2:9). Now Luke declares in Acts that God made Jesus both Lord and Christ. Yet in making Jesus Lord and as Christ, giving Him preeminence, God did not do it simply because He was His only begotten Son. To do so would be nepotism plain and simple, which is the promoting of someone simply because they are a relative.

This notion is not uncommon to most. Some may even have been the victims of nepotism. For example, on the job you may be the one with the skill and the maturity to complete assignments, or perhaps in the church you may be the one with the anointing upon your life for ministry. Nevertheless, because you're not the son or daughter of the man in charge you may be overlooked and your position given to a member of the family. This was not the case with God and His Son! Jesus Christ had an awesome responsibility given to Him before the foundations of the world. He completed the job all the way to the cross of Calvary but it was not over until He ascended and appeared before God after His resurrection, showing God that, as His Son, He had completed the assignment as both sacrificial Lamb and High Priest. (*ref.* Saint John 20:17) Therefore, ***"It pleased the Father that in Him (Christ) should all the fullness of the godhead dwell bodily."*** (*ref.* Colossians 2:9) This is why in our worship, praise, and songs of adoration we can declare and proclaim that Jesus Christ alone is *worthy*! Just to think it all began in "the mind of Christ."

Hence, if we are indeed going to serve God at all that too must start with our minds. Therefore, we must become more protective of our thoughts and mental energies. Not only must we guard ourselves from carnal thoughts which seek to find their way into our deeds but we must also guard our minds from the pains of worry and fretting which can filter into our spirits and emotions.

It takes Time To Worry

YOU MAY ASK, "How in fact does worry affect my stewardship habits?" The answer is simple: Worrying burns up and utilizes good, mental energy. This is mental energy that could have been utilized in envisioning and subsequently doing something good and purposeful for the Lord and others. Contemplation is defined in a few words as "to consider, study, examine, scrutinize . . . " Once contemplation grips the mind, individuals can consequently find themselves engaged in abstract thought for dangerously long periods of time. Often when this happens it becomes difficult for that individual to engage in any constructive thought or productive activity without concurrently worrying. "In contrast to nonworriers, chronic worriers spend up to eight hours a day fretting, and this fretting disrupts their lives and is clearly seen as a problem. In addition, worriers report being more anxious, tense, apprehensive, physically upset, depressed, obsessive and publicly self-conscious than nonworriers."[3]

We will address these and other effects later in the book, but if we could only see the enormous investment of time worry requires we could avoid its devastating effects. Don't fool yourself; it takes time to worry and time is valuable! The older one becomes the more he realizes he must become a better steward of his time. Although this stewardship may cause some to consider you intolerant or short of patience you must insist that time is important and you really don't have time to waste!

Solomon told us, ***"To everything there is a season, and a time under the heaven..."*** (*ref.* Ecclesiastes 3:1-9) When we consider that every season is dedicated to a specific purpose we realize there is no time to waste. Even if we take time to rest and relax we must understand there is a time for this and we should not feel guilty for taking it. Not having this understanding will cause us to avoid vacations, to miss quality time with our families and friends and create for ourselves needless anxiety along with other more serious health problems.

How many marriages are affected because upwardly-mobile individuals and workaholics don't know when to stop work and go home and relax? We hear dozens of sermons about reaching our destiny and fulfilling our purpose, but if we don't spend time with our families in settings where our vocation is not the preeminent issue, we will never reach our destiny. Purpose should never come at the expense of our families. The failure to realize this fact has become the major source of resentment many family members have towards the ministry.

So often people in ministry lose the best years of quality relationship with their spouses and children attempting to care for Christ's church all in the name of ministry. We devote inordinate amounts of time trying to make a name for ourselves doing things that, perhaps, God never told us to do. Right now I'm talking especially to pastors and ministry-workers. We really can't manage the affairs of the church with a caretaker mentality; watching over things, which are not in our control anyway!

> ***"Except the Lord builds the house, they labor in vain who build it; except the Lord keeps the city, the watchman, wakest but in vain. It is vain for you to rise up early, to take rest late, to eat the bread of [anxious] toil..."*** (Psalm 127:1-2)

I've discovered it's better to live an example before the people, preach, teach, and then allow the Holy Spirit to do His job. For it is the work of the Holy Ghost to lead, guide, and to develop the Word preached into the spirits of men once the sermon is over. When I've done my job and know the Lord is pleased I take my wife and family and go somewhere and relax—trusting that God is far better able than I am to take care of *'the Church'* (for whom He died)!

If you are one of those persons who feels as though this book is not for you but you admit to carrying your cell phone on vacation with you, you should think again. We really don't have time to worry about anything that will eventually be taken care of *in time!* One thing I've discovered is that time is a revealer. If we allow time to take its course and try not to make things happen before their time we would learn to live more stress-free and purpose-driven lives.

Once you master this, you can vacate and rest without a cell phone at your side. You can take your mind off cares without feeling guilty. Moreover, you must realize your congregation needs you to exemplify these principles for them and their families almost as much as they need you behind the pulpit.

Jesus Used His Time Wisely

CAN YOU IMAGINE how much of Jesus' time during His three and a half years of ministry would have been wasted had He worried about all of the issues and matters of importance which confronted Him? Being God and being able to do anything, He could addressed any and all the ills of the world, especially those which He personally encountered. After all He is all-knowing and omnipotent, but He had a purpose and He remained focused. Even though there aren't enough volumes of books to record all of His deeds there were still many things which He simply did not address. He was a man with a mission. Christ knew the time allotted to Him and with all of his responsibilities He found time to rest, vacate and spend quality time with those closest to Him-- even when His rest was interrupted by either the multitude who sought after Him or by faithless disciples worried about impending danger. (*ref.* Saint Mark 4:38)

What a tremendous lesson to those of us who minister! Jesus maximized His personal time and revolutionized the world for His era and for all ages to come. Remember that, before all else, His mind-set was to do the will of His Father. He remained focused because He not only knew who He was but He always remembered what He had come to do. He did not hesitate to remind those closest to Him of that fact. With Jesus having thousands thronging Him, and disciples and others suggesting possibilities which were more self-serving than divinely inspired, Jesus had to remain fully surrendered to the will of God in order to stay on task.

If we would free ourselves of distractions, our prayers would be more Christ-centered and focused. Consequently, there would be little prayer-time wasted attempting to undo what should never have been done if we had only waited on God, sought His will and obeyed His voice.

In most pastoral counseling sessions many of the things people rehearse in their discourse are situations where they moved too fast because they were worried about their future and some impending outcome. Sadly, when they are confronted with biblical solutions intended to equip them with tools to address their problem many would rather continue rehearsing the problem than appropriate the Word of God for a solution. This often happens because most aren't ready to accept the Word's challenges as the final authority.

Paul said ***"I couldn't talk to you as spiritual because you are carnal."*** (*ref.* 1 Corinthians 3:1) In other words, Paul was saying, "I want to give you the challenge of spiritual responsibility and watch you obey but you are too carnal-minded to respond appropriately." When we are lead by the Spirit, we will mind the things of the Spirit. But when we are fleshly we will mind the things of the flesh.

The Bible provides practical answers to life's problems, but it will not do the task for us. It makes us responsible for what we have read and know. Once we know what God says, we must then become doers of the Word and not hearers only. We should be aware, however, that failure to read the Word does not exempt us nor give us an excuse simply because we don't know. Some even devalue their time in the Word because they don't want to accept the responsibility for what they have read. Still, we are held responsible and this kind of ignorance will not exempt us but will ultimately cause our own destruction. Hence, much of what some would call counseling is really a waste of valuable time because many of these people have not sought the Wonderful Counselor, Jesus Christ, the only wise God our Savior.

Time Is A Revealer

SOMETHING ELSE to consider is that we must beware of those to whom we give our time to. There are some people who have a demonic assignment to rob others of their destiny. They have been unleashed to distract you and keep you from fulfilling your goals. Although this is virtually a mission impossible, it is nonetheless their purpose. I've come to realize that it is a demonic spirit! Many times people appear on the surface as though they are genuinely seeking direction, relationship, and covenant. However, time will reveal that their true assignment is really to divert your attention.

Once you truly realize you only have so much time to achieve your purpose and destiny, you will become more guarded, focused, and watchful. The Bible says, ***"Know them that labor among you..."*** (*ref.* 1 Thessalonians 5:12) Allow time to work in your best interest. Remember time is a revealer. Nothing will show you some things like time. When people show you who they really are believe them. Some people are showing you that their only purpose in life is to negatively affect people of purpose. Some of you may think it's too late, but you can recover! Thank God we serve a merciful Savior who declares that our life and times are in *His* hand. Therefore, our pains, hurts, disappointments, and shortcomings are all working for our good.

One of the things we must realize about the enemy is the ***"thief cometh but for to steal..."*** (*ref.* Saint John 10:10) He desires to steal not only our finances, health, prosperity and families, he also desires to steal our time! Even satan knows time is winding up. Just knowing that there is a time to die, and to kill, to weep and to mourn; a time to lose, to hate and to war should help us accept the fact that there are some things we cannot change. Even these negative things of life have an allotted time for their existence. By accepting this facts of life we free ourselves from worrying about the inevitable. The knowledge that even negative things of life has an allotted time should help us handle them when they arrive. We should remember, just as they are destined to come, they also have a determined end. Just as in life we have death; and through death life is regenerated--so does the negative aspects of life produce positive outcomes if we would only allow them. Having this understanding will not only help us handle the crisis when they come, it will teach us how to live life to its fullest.

This is why the Word is so important for the believer because it answers all the issues of life and enables us to better enjoy the good times—those times of health, laughter, dancing, reaping, love and times of peace. Like it or not troubles will come! But they do not have to rob us of our appreciation of the quality of life. This is how we can live even in the valley of death. I've discovered that by economizing my thoughts and freeing myself of worry I'm able to add to my good times.

Good News For Bad Times

LIKE OR NOT, the time to die is ever approaching. The reality is, in the natural or fleshly realm we are all at the mercy of death's allotted time. Death has been allotted its season. It is the last enemy to be destroy, and it has no sting for the born again child of God. Nonetheless, we are still made subject to it allotted time. This is why we all grow older, our eyes are getting dimmer, and our bodies are subject to the effects of death. The Bible admonishes us on how to respond to the process of death.

> ***"Lord teach us to number our days that we may apply our hearts to wisdom"*** (*ref.* Psalms 90:12)

It is this wisdom which comes from a relationship with God through Jesus Christ that allows us to understand, that "though our outward man perish, the inward man is renewed daily..." (*ref.* 2 Corinthians 4:16) Through eternal life we are in the process of life and not death. Therefore things which only have validity within the short-term temporal realm of this earth should not worry and perplex us since we don't have to live here forever. As a child of God one can detract from their bad times by not giving in to them, always knowing that just as God orders the blessings which come in our lives He also preserves the same over the storms of life. It is God who *"changeth the times and seasons"* of our destiny. (*ref.* Daniel 2:21) I've learned, as a believer, to find good news from God's Word especially concerning your bad times. This will allow you to keep abounding, in spite of the pressures which attempt to keep you down!

What is it that God has to say to you concerning the things that you are experiencing now? Has He given you a rhema, a sure and direct word that your test is only for a season? Having a rhema word from the Lord about your problems and dilemmas puts you in control of situations so they won't control you. When a rhema or a prophetic word comes grab a hold of it and retain it through the tough seasons of life. God sends us messages in various forms to sustain us through the night. These are the tools to equip believers and nonworriers to make the best of their time. Faithful nonworriers know how to be instant in season and out of season, and to always abound even when they've been counted out. Ultimately they learn to be content in *whatsoever* state they're in. For worriers, even when their good times come they rob *themselves* and their quality of life by worrying when they should be enjoying life as it is. No wonder Paul said, ***"I've learned in whatsoever I'm in therewith to be content."*** (*ref.* Philippians 4:11)

Hence, as a praiser, I have learned to capitalize upon this principle. Being able to enter a realm of praise and worship helped me to be content with the things I can't change. David said, ***"I will bless the Lord at all times, and His praise shall continually be in my mouth."*** (*ref.* Psalm 34:1) This is what I call time-stewardship! Don't be caught with your works undone simply because there are things and people working against. You only have an allotted amount of time. Don't waste it worrying. To do so would be irresponsible.

4

A MEANS TO AN END

"From God's perspective, what you have need of is the end of the matter and your promise is only a means to His end."

WHENEVER ONE believes God for a promise that individual tends to think of the promise as an end within itself. For example, one may pray, "Lord You promised You would provide the job, companionship, the car, or peace of mind;" and there are those instances that God actually makes these types of promises. Even when you have this kind of promise you can easily become so focused on the it that you lose sight of what *God* actually wants out of the transaction. In the scenario, God is saying, "you may want the promise, but you have *'need'* of something else. Although I may provide for your desires I have knowledge of some greater needs you are not aware of." *He sees the need, we see the promise.* Most think that once the promise is received that is the end of the matter. It certainly is not!

From God's perspective what you have need of is the end

of the matter and your promise is only a means to His end. Consider what the writer of Hebrews says, ***"Cast not away therefore your confidence, which has great recompense of reward. For ye have need of patience that, after ye have done the will of God ye might receive the promise."*** (*ref.* chp. 10, vs. 35-36) Besides your promise or desire there are two primary things involved in the divine arrangement of human provisions. There is *"the will of God"* and in this case the *"patience"* which you *"have need of."* Therefore, the promise is the means by which the end is achieved.

If you've ever made impulsive mistakes and have had to pray to God for forgive, to undo those things which only He can handle, you soon learn how to wait on Him and trust His perfect wisdom. It is the waiting, in spite of the odds, which develops the patience we need--thereby giving solace to our anxious wills. This is why, like Paul, we ultimately ***"glory in tribulations also: knowing that tribulation worketh patience; and patience, experience."*** (*ref.* Romans 5:3) Consequently, the character development that is derived from our test is far greater than our request; and, those negative, painful situations worked for our good because we love God and are called according to His purpose. (*ref.* Romans 8:28)

Seeking His Face Not His Hand

ONE CAN ONLY ARRIVE at this revelation when he understand that the most important thing for the child of God is to seek the *face* of God and not His *hand.* At the hand of God, we seek what we believe to be the blessings of God. As a result, we have become too concerned with what we perceive to be blessings. We must understand that *"blessed"* is mainly translated *"happy or happiness."* Often if we aren't given a sermon of promises and tangible blessings we feel as though we've been cheated. Accordingly, preachers have programmed their sermons to conclude with some sort of guaranteed blessing to the people. As a result many people aren't seeking after the face of God where His mind and will are revealed. They seek only His hand. And for many, if God was to withdraw His hand many people would withdraw themselves. The truth is, God is more interested in us *being* a blessing than *having* a blessing. We must understand that others are to be blessed as a result of their contact with us.

What we have confused with the blessings of the Lord are His provisions. Many of the provisions of God are materialistic or tangible in nature, but materialistic blessings are usually the last thing God provides and this is for good reason. One reason for this is that when we believe God for a provisional promise there is always something more we are in *need* of besides the promise. This is why the writer of Hebrews told us, ***"Do not, therefore, fling away your fearless confidence, for it carries a great and glorious compensation of reward."*** (*ref.* Hebrews 10:35-36, AMP) The other reason God waits before providing the promise is because He does not want His material blessings to be confused with material things obtained by other means.

Material possessions can be easily duplicated by other sources, including one's self and even the devil. But the difference with God is that ***"... the blessings of the Lord maketh rich and addeth no sorrow with it."*** (*ref.* Proverbs 10:22) Hear what David said about the treasured presence of the Almighty God, ***"You have said, Seek you My face—inquire for and require My presence [as your vital need]. My heart says to You, Your face [Your presence], Lord, will I seek..."*** (*ref.* Psalm 27:8, AMP) Therefore, it is God's ultimate desire that we seek His face, where the presence of His character resides, so that His blessings will be upon us, both spiritually and naturally.

Stay Focused for Effective Ministry

SAD TO SAY, this pre-occupation with the hand of God has found its way even into the hearts of many leaders in one form or another. Many even worry about missing their chance and place in ministry. They see the clock ticking or observe others as they are being used and their ministries advancing and soon they begin to ask, "What about me... Don't I have ministry within me…? Don't I matter to God?" Questions like these are pondered in the minds of men and women if not verbalized everyday. People want to know "What's my lot?" Often this occurs because even in the Church we are made to feel the competitive pressures of the "mega-church" syndrome, when every church or pastor is clearly not called to this assignment or mission. The competitive rat-race of ministry have dampened the love of genuine relationships among Christian brethren of like faith. The fact is that only purpose and effectiveness can measure one's success.

I must confess I've been there and felt the pressure. But I remember a passage of scripture the Lord brought to my attention during one of those periods. Saint John 21:20-22 (NKJV) says, ***"Then Peter, turning around, saw the disciple (speaking of John), whom Jesus loved following... Peter seeing him said to Jesus, But Lord, what about this man? Jesus said to him, If I will that he remain till I come, what is that to you? You follow thou Me."*** Here's what happened. In this story Jesus had just told Peter about the end of his ministry and what type of death he would experience. Peter knowing how Jesus loved John and seeing John he asked, "Well, how about him?" Jesus' simple reply to Peter, was "Don't worry about John, you stay focused! If I never allow John to see death and he remain until I come again, what is that to you Peter?"

If the Lord has ever chastened you then you know a real rhema when you hear one. At the moment I read that passage it was as if Jesus had spoken directly to me, saying, *Why are you worried about how I am using someone else, and other ministries around you... If I chose to uniquely use them from now until I come, what is that to you? Just stay focused upon what has been assigned to your hands!* This began to remind me of what He had promised me. My admonishment was to, *Do what I've told you to do and stay focused. Your current test and suffering is only a means to accomplish a predetermined end!* He assured me that He was able to perform all He had promised. I took my rebuke and moved on with my assignment, being happy I was even chosen to be apart of His divine program.

Can't you see how easy it is to get out of the will of God? It can all begin with something as simple as worrying. It doesn't matter how trivial the worries are just as long as they are distractive. Hence, worry will cause you to wander, and once you start wandering in your mind, and continue long enough, you will stray from your task and purpose. How many of us are busy doing things simply because we are worried about impressing someone else or keeping up with some other ministry? Projects, no matter how benevolent, must be filtered through God's will. I've concluded that I don't want to hear God say to me, You and your church have had some good projects...you impressed your community, the city officials and your peers, but I was not impressed... You went to conferences and conventions, bragging about what you're doing in your home town and how many folks you have... but you have abandoned what I told you to do!

Countless individuals have strayed away from their assignments worrying about what impact someone else is making or if their own ministry is making an impact at all. This is the only century many of us will ever see and I'm confident that we won't see another millennium until *Thee Millennium.* This is the season to do whatever we are going to do for God and to make our main concern hearing Him say, ***"Well done good and faithful servant..."*** (*ref.* Saint Matthew 25:21)

Guilty of Doing Nothing

THERE IS ONE MORE observation we need to consider regarding time-stewardship. Not only are there more constructive things that can be done in the time wasted worrying there is something else more serious to consider. Did you know poor time-stewardship feeds the sin of omission? And the sin of omission is something we can commit without really thinking about it. I will never forget a hallmark sermon preached by my mentor and father-in-law, the late Bishop Winfield Showell, called *"The Sin of Omission."* In that message he described how many believers will one day come before God and hear Him charge them with the crime of having *done nothing.* That is what happened to the man who had the one talent! Because he was worried about unimportant things he buried his talent, rested on his laurels, and did nothing. (*ref.* Saint Matthew 25:14-30) He even attempted to argue that his worries were well-founded because the lord of the harvest was a *"hard taskmaster,"* as if to justify his functioning-fears. This servant thought that would excuse his deliberate inactivity. He thought he was shrewd, but Jesus called him *"wicked!"*

If we don't keep our mind on the fact that God has given us a stewardship responsibility we too will bury our gifts in the sands and will have reproduced nothing at His coming. Jesus said, ***"many will say to Me in that day, Lord, Lord, have***

we not prophesied in thy name and in thy name cast out devils and in thy name done many wonderful works?" (*ref.* Saint Matthew 7:22) The only way to be productive is to use everything God has given us. We must use our creativity if we are going to be faithful, industrious, stewards in this day of high technology and proficiency. Our minds must be free and clear of all the negative clutter and anti-productive thoughts which become lethal, self-made tools in the hand of an enemy who wants to defeat us and cause us to fail God. With minds free of envious worry we can truly hear from God.

No Comparison

LET ME SHARE a situation that occurred in the early stages of my pastorate. Hopefully it will help someone see one of satan's devices for what it is. I was teaching a study series on spiritual gifts. Over the course of the lessons I decided to give the entire church a spiritual-gifts inventory which evaluated where each member's gifts were. As the church was completing the evaluation everyone was excited and things seemed to be going well. I collected the sheets and announced that the results would be available by the next week's Bible class. Well, it was not until the next week that I became so frustrated that I almost regret ever approaching the subject.

As the individual members began to review their results and we began discussing the various gift categories people found themselves in, a few people suddenly began to complain. They began to compare their *"assumed"* or *"supposed"* spiritual gifts to others. I heard complaints like, "I'm really a prophet or teacher... how did she get to be that? ...This test can't be right..." When I asked how many had answered the battery of questions truthfully, everyone raised their hands.

It was explained that the results could only be determined

by the answers people had provided, that it was not a conclusive test and that it in no ways concluded what anyone would ultimately become. I explained that whether or not an individual ultimately exemplifies these gifts is based upon many other spiritual factors and that this instrument was only an evaluation tool. In other words, it was only a means to an end! Still because of the immaturity and covetousness of some individuals I had to remind the church that we are all called according to the hope of Christ's calling. He has distributed to each of us a measure of faith and He knows what we need for us to get whatever assigned job done for Him.

I again reminded them of the three stewards in Jesus' story--that it is Christ who gave every man according to his ability. Some in the church at that time became spiritually "stuck" because they only saw themselves one way and refused to use the talents they had to produce anything more for God. Better still, they refused to go through the process necessary for God to develop them in the areas they desired. Consequently, this led some self-willed people to scamper to find venuses where those talents they felt best described them could be utilized. According to the Bible, their behavior was not considered "striving lawfully". We have become a generation like Peter(s)--too focused on John!

Use What You've Got

WE ALL HAVE SOMETHING to give to the Body of Christ. It is irresponsible of any of us to compare ourselves to others or feel we have nothing to give. To feel this way is to claim that God didn't give you anything and that isn't true. The Bible says, ***"He who descended is also he that also ascended and lead into captivity and gave gifts to men."*** (*ref.* Ephesians 4:10) He is the Lord of the harvest and we, as His stewards, are left to occupy until He comes. You must become perfect. And in this context perfect actually means ripened, like good fruit. Just because, at times, you may feel as though you don't have what others have, doesn't mean you won't be called into account for what you possess. Your possession will generate your fruit. The warning is, *"Don't be irresponsible!"* Stop wasting time! Stop telling God, and others, you don't know what your calling is. Dig up the buried talents you have! The Lord of the harvest is coming. We must ***"work while it is day for night cometh and no man can work."*** (*ref.* Saint John 9:4)

Can't you see that the night of our age is upon us? Everything around us is declaring that Jesus is coming soon. I believe it is much sooner than we think! This sobering reality constrains us to weigh everything in terms of God's kingdom and His will for our lives. There is a promise of entering into His rest for all who labor. The imminent return of Christ is that promised rest which all believers await. If we are to indeed obtain that rest we must fight to win it. Fighting those attacks which are assailed at us and fight just as aggressively those thoughts which rise within us.

There are combative elements in life which we all face, but we can't sit, do nothing and expect to hear Christ say, ***"Well done"*** when He returns (*ref.* Saint Matthew 25:21). Remember the promised rest is the end, but your labor is the means to the end. Only the responsible steward can enter into the rest of God. This rest will begin the moment we're freed from needless worry and exhibit a worry-free trust in God which inevitably brings peace to our minds.

5

DIVINE SOLUTIONS OVER HUMAN ANSWERS

"Once you learn to relish the sweet taste of God's peace, you will avoid those hasty decisions which end up being objects of your future prayers."

ONE OF THE THINGS which makes life so interesting is the fact that there is variety and diversity to life. Additionally, there is normalcy and there are extremes. Any discussion of the subject of normalcy would necessitate a book all by itself. However, it is necessary to discuss extremes as it relates to worry. Extremes are those things that exceed ordinary or usual expectancy. They are found at the farthest possible point from the middle. Most people find a happy median for their daily existence, which is that central point. If we consider the subject of worry as it relates to extremism, we will see that there are those who find themselves at either the middle or end of the spectrum. On one hand, we find the average worriers, who worries but is able to come to a decision and act. On the other hand we have the chronic worriers would sooner become paralyzed than make a move. The chronic worrier would be considered extreme, though all chronic worriers are not immobile. You also have those who, because of chronic worry, are so impulsive he seem to get ahead of himself and God in a compulsive need to do something-- anything! Impulsivity may produce action, but most often it causes many regrets over the action taken or the outcome it produces. While you don't want to be stalemated in your worrisome reluctance, you also don't want to be irrational and presumptuous. Both extremes demonstrate a lack of faith. As a child of God, your life must become so Christ-*centered* until there is little room left for either of these extremes. To begin you must evaluate your actions, plans and thoughts to see if they are in the will of God.

The truth of the matter is that many of the things we worry about are things we have not originally handled according to God's Word. The Bible says, ***"Be careful (anxious) for nothing; but in everything by prayer and supplication with thanksgiving, let your requests be made known unto God."*** And as a result, ***"...the peace of God, which passes all understanding, shall keep [guard, preserve, maintain, support and protect] your hearts and minds through Christ Jesus."*** (*ref.* Philippians 4:6-7). Isaiah wrote a "Song of Salvation" which says, ***"I will keep you in perfect peace whose mind is stayed on me... because you trust in Me."*** (*ref.* vs. 20:3) If there is any one thing both impulsiveness and worrying have in common it is that they both will rob you of God's peace. They operate at different rates of speed and at different times, but their end is the same.

This peace the Master promises is worth more than all the

material things in the world. It's a peace that is not shaken by external or internal circumstances. If you have ever experienced a time where your mind was so full of unrest that even your sleep was threatened by images of impending or perceived danger, then you'd know the value of peace! Psalms 37:37 says, ***"Mark the perfect man, and behold the upright; for the end of that man is peace."*** No matter what befalls you, you should not allow it to rob you of the very thing that should portray you as a child of God: His abundant peace. It's a part of the children's bread! Once you learn to relish the sweet taste of God's peace you will avoid those hasty decisions which end up being objects of your future prayers.

Don't Settle for Second Best

I HAD AN EXPERIENCE with God, which left an indelible print on my mind. I was driving to an undergraduate class one day at a local college. While driving down a street I had traveled on many occasions, I looked at a housing development that I once considered for my family. What had originally attracted me to that development was its billboard advertising its low financing and easy access. What really motivated my interest in this property, however, was not the easy accessibility but the pressure I felt to move my family into our own home. Yet here I was, two years later, sitting in my car waiting for the light to change, and in front of my face was this development which had become so devastatingly poor that I thought, "Just think, I almost moved here!"

Immediately I heard the voice of the Lord, which spoke so clearly, saying, *"You were willing to settle for that place, but that was not the place I had for you... Look at where you're living now! Isn't it just what your heart desired? Look at the car you're driving. I gave you this car... Look at the school you're attending, it's one of the top colleges in the country… I did it! Why are you so quick to settle for less than what I wanted to give you? Why do you give in under pressure of other people's opinions? I've always wanted more for you than you often wanted for yourself… And if you trust Me, I will fulfill all of My goodwill concerning you."*

By the time I reached my destination I was crying and praising God so much that I had to slip into the restroom to regroup before going to class. That day God dealt so intimately with me about my impulsivity versus my level of trust in Him.

He showed me the gross inconveniences of my life caused by moving ahead of Him, often motivated by what people thought rather than by my own knowledge of what God thought of me. That day the Lord added new meaning to the passage, which says, ***"…I know My thoughts that I think toward you, saith the Lord, thoughts of peace, and not of evil, to give you an expected end."*** (*ref.* Jeremiah 29:11) Not only did this scripture become a lamp to my feet as He guided me out of the valley of despair, but I came to understand the unchangeable fact that I do have an expected end which has already been predestined by God.

The Lord gave me a new understanding of delayed gratification: *Delay is not denial* and the lack of discipline in this area, is in fact a lack of faith. Impulsiveness tells you, "I must have it now because there may never be a later!" But faith says, "The God of my today(s) is also the God of my tomorrow(s). ***"And though it tarries I will wait for it… and when it arrives it will not lie!"*** (*ref.* Habakkuk 2:3) For God is in control of my expected end. He showed me the link between worrying about self-image and what others think and how it connected with poor decisions and actions. We must all come to a place where our trust in God becomes so firm that even if we are misunderstood we must hold fast to the confession of our faith. That's the trust He's looking for and His promised peace will comes as a result. Ultimately, His peace exceeds *all our* understanding! (*ref.* Philippians 4:7)

Once we have made our requests known to God, we must trust and believe Him for the results, giving Him thanks for the resolution. We should also understand that His resolution may or may not be the answer we are looking for. Thanking God for the resolution of a problem is quite different from thanking Him for the answer. This is because so often we already have a desired answer in mind while we are praying. This point is important. You see, if we don't resign ourselves to the fact that His resolution may not be our resolution, just as His ways are not our ways, nor His thoughts our thoughts, we will unknowingly provide the safe passage of worry and its characteristics into our prayer life.

Proper Reaction for Improper Actions

DAVID PROVIDES FOR US a beautiful illustration of how not to allow this to happen. This illustration is perfect because many people are dealing with the results of bad decisions, poor judgments, gross sin and even feelings of failure. Some may be asking, "What do I do when I've already made the wrong decision, moved out of haste and am now facing the results of having failed God? How do I trust God in a mess I've caused?"

Remember when David sinned with Bathsheba, Uriah's wife? He forgot the importance of who he was and allowed the pressures of leadership to be soothed by his fleshly emotions and undisciplined spirit. David further added to his sin by having Uriah killed once he discovered Bathsheba was pregnant with his child (*ref.* 2 Samuel 11:1; 14:33). The crisis of the moment dictated his subsequent behavior. In his impulsiveness, he responded by acting outside of God's will, standards, and divine expectation. Afterward the prophet Nathan confronted David, bringing him to a place of profound repentance. Even after he and Bathsheba thought they could go on with their lives and live happily ever after, there came a day of reckoning once the baby was born, and David found himself a victim of perplexity. If you've ever dealt with having to face God's impending judgment for a sin you committed, then you can imagine David's dilemma. His love child was born and this innocent baby was immediately summoned to die as a result of the sins of his father.

Nonetheless during the child's sickness David fasted and prayed, hoping for a reprieve. David was so distraught during his vexation period until the elders of the land didn't want to approach him with the news that the *"answer"* he'd so desperately sought was not God's ultimate will. The child indeed died! This was God's divine solution to David's problem. I'm sure David imagined many ways God could have solved the problem without killing his child. We too have many things we want spared, but many of the things we want spared are actually the things we must allow God to kill before they ultimately kill us! These issues are birth out of our lack of faith, trust and obedience. Abram's lack of trust birth Ishmael, the child of bondage. And Ishmael is still attempting to kill Isaac (the Israelites), the child of promise to this very day. The Bible is full of illustrations to this fact. It's all a matter of man's will versus God's will. Divine solution over man's answers.

Worship Beyond Disappointments

THE BEAUTIFUL THING about David's story is found in 2 Samuel 12:19, 20 which says, ***"But when David saw that his servants whispered, David perceived that the child was dead:***

therefore David said unto his servants, is the child dead? And they said, 'He is dead'. Then David arose from the earth, and washed, and anointed himself, and changed his apparel, and came into the house of the Lord, and worshiped." David resigned himself to God's sovereign resolution even when it was not the preferred answer he desired. Ultimately, he was able to worship beyond his disappointment. There is a level of faith we can attain that suffices for anything else we could desire. Just as sure as there is life after death, there is worship after disappointment! For David, just knowing that he was still in God's plan was a satisfying resolution, which was far more than he deserved. David didn't allow the difference between *God's sovereign will* and *his self-centered desires* to rob him from his relationship with God. I believe David was grateful that he was still able to claim a relationship with God. Therefore, he used his experience to bring himself closer to God! His submission made a happy ending out of what could have been a devastating disaster.

When the results of our problems, or better yet, the fruit of our doings do not produce the outcomes we desire, we must not only refrain from worry, but we must resolve ourselves to accept God's will without becoming indifferent or bitter. This is important because it is during times of reckoning that the devil speaks to us about all the ramifications which may have lead to our problem. The adversary wants us to point fingers at others or retaliate, hurting those who have caused us hurt, but we must maintain an honest and pure heart with God so our prayer will not be hindered. We must pray as David prayed in Psalms 51. The first thing he did to protect his relationship with God was to acknowledge that the sin he'd committed was against God and God only. In verse 3-4, he says, ***"For I acknowledge my transgressions, and my sin is always before me. Against You, and You only have I sinned and done***

this evil in Your sight—that You may be found just when You speak and blameless when You judge." (NKJV).

Once worry crosses over into our prayers the end result is that we become too focused on an expected outcome or a desired end. When this occurs the words of our supplication transcend into a litany of worries. In essence we are not praying we are actually articulating to God those things we earnestly desire. In these kind of prayers we're not *truly* exercising faith according to His will. This turns our prayer into a severe list of concerns or simply a *"wants-list."* Consequently, our prayers are incomplete because praying this way leaves little room for thanksgiving. Additionally, thanksgiving, in lieu of worrying, can only be accomplished when there is trust. When we sincerely thank God in advance we are saying in short, "I trust Your wisdom and grace in knowing what is best for me… I thank You for the outcome."

Let's face it, it takes faith to trust many of God's consequences. It is our thanksgiving in worship that ushers us into the presence of God. For it is there that He exposes us to another aspect of His character and nature, which makes our wants and desires pale in comparison. The Bible says, ***"...In everything give thanks for this is the will of God in Christ Jesus concerning you."*** (*ref.* 1 Thessalonians 5:18) Worry will not allow you to thank God, especially *for* some things, but trust will allow you to thank God *in* everything. There's an old song we sometimes sing called, "Take Your Burdens to the Lord and Leave Them There." It is important in supplication that we leave our petitions with God.

God wants our spirits and minds free. It takes more than just singing about freedom from sin and the bondage of the enemy. If we are truly saved and free from sin then this life of freedom includes God's provisions for keeping our minds free of the clutter of common worry. Remember that you must be free in your spirit to appropriately worship. By doing so your worship will keep you in God's will while you await His divine outcome.

Knowing God has an expected end, which is His sovereign solution according to His will, should grant us peace and assure us of our purpose. His involvement in our affairs reminds us that God is so much in control that He will not allow our circumstances to consume us, nor our enemies to triumph over us. There is nothing greater than God's will! We all know the power of man's will in relationship to his accomplishments. Mortal man has proven, and God has testified, that nearly nothing is impossible for man once his mental will is stirred. Just to think, the great God, Creature of everything can employ His awesome will to set our destinies securely in place, will shake the heavens and the earth to bring it to pass. It really makes you wonder, what is man that God thinks so much of him? (*ref.* Psalm 8:4; *ff.* Hebrews 2:6)

Once God wills something for your lives all of the demons in hell cannot stop or hinder the will of God! As one who has personally experienced God's grace in this area, I command you right now in the Name of Jesus Christ to lift up your head, strengthen *"the feeble knee, lift up the hands which hang down"* and worship! (*ref.* Hebrews 12:12) In fact, God will actually ***"prepare a table before you in the presence of your enemies."*** (*ref.* Psalms 23:5) That's all a part of His divine resolution. This is why we can't evaluate an individual according to his circumstances, nor determine what God thinks of an individual relevant to his problem or conditions. We must be very careful who we talk about when voicing our opinions of others! It's not over until God says its over!

We don't know how God is using those negative events in an individual's life to bring him closer to His will. Would it be better that we not experience bad situations as a result of bad choices or judgement? Yes, of course! The truth is, God knows how we will ultimately respond to pressure. He knows if we will maintain the integrity of His name or not. He knows those whom He has chosen, ***"...for many are called but few are chosen."*** (ref. Saint Matthew 20:16) The chosen are those who said, "I can't take no more" but they took it; or said, "I can't go on" but found the strength to go on! He knows whether or not we will faint or run in escape. Proverbs 24:10 says, ***"If thou faint in the day of adversity thy strength is small."*** God will not give big things to people of small strength and little faith.

Celebrating Survival

CELEBRATE THE JOY of knowing that you are still here because you had strength to survive. Everything around you was pointing towards your death. Even those people who you thought were your friends pronounced "ashes to ashes and dust to dust" over you. But having obtained help from God you've continued until this day! That's because you are a survivor! The enemy wants you worrying when you should be celebrating survival! If you are going to begin to live worry-free, then you must become confident of God's thoughts concerning you. God's thoughts sealed His sovereign will for your life. Even your failures will work out for your good. Although you may bear marks of your suffering, God is still faithful to perform His good word towards you.

Accept the fact that God's ways of working things out are not always going to be as you desire. He does love you with an everlasting love. Therefore, He *will* perform everything after the counsel of *His own will*. Learning to live with this assurance will grant you a life of peace, godly-contentment and great gain.

6

A MATTER OF REVERENCE

" . . . To worry is to show irreverence towards God. By persistent worry, we are actually saying we don't really trust God."

UNBELIEF, manifested by perplexity and severe contemplation, reveals the third aspect of worry I wish to discuss. This degree of worry may be difficult for many worshiping-believers to consider or accept. This is due largely to the fact that the average Christian considers himself to be respectful towards God. No true believer wants to be of the opinion that he is contrary where his trust in God and respect for Him are concerned. Nevertheless, while developing our faith-walk with God there is a form of disrespect we must all honestly confront as we strive to please Him.

The truth is, worrying shows irreverence towards God. By persistent worry we are actually saying we don't really trust God. Feelings of mistrust should be reserved for characters of low moral fiber, such as liars, thieves and the unethical. Anything and anyone we fear and respect, we should reverence. As natural and typical as it may seem to be in our everyday lives, worry is a matter of disrespect towards God. When we worry about how to handle a situation we show a lack of confidence, which is also a lack of faith, in God. Let me be the first to admit that we are all faced with circumstances which, at first, may appear to be impossible or at least uncertain. But that is never the end of the story where God is concerned.

There are some things we really can't handle by ourselves and there's no harm in admitting it. Once we admit it, the next step is to give it over to the Lord, allowing Him to be LORD in whatever it is. It is only through His lordship that we discover His sovereignty and absolute rulership over crises. Even if God doesn't operate in a manner which makes sense to us we must surrender absolute trust and confidence in Him and try not to interfere with His ways or methods. You see, by worrying, we are actually saying, "Well, since God hasn't come up with a solution then *I'll* have to ponder in my finite mind all possible answers until *I* can find the best remedy." Let's face it, we do behave as if we know as much as God does, or as if our ways are equal to His infinite ways.

Though we dare not verbalize nor admit to such thoughts we *do think* like this and that is disrespectful, plain and simple! Isn't it strange how we can trust and believe God to manage the universe, the rising and setting of the sun, the orderly rotation of the seasons, controlling the very existence of life, but yet we behave as if our world is too complex for Him to manage without *our* assistance? This is another form of the creature instructing the Creator, or the pot telling the Potter how he ought to be made. This kind of thinking is also the stimulus for impulsive behavior and is motivated by a lack of faith.

Let's face it, without faith it is impossible to even please God not to mention respect Him: ***"for he that cometh to God must believe that He is, and that He is a rewarder of them that diligently seek Him."*** (*ref.* Hebrew 11:6). The operative word is diligently, which means seeking Him persistently, unrelentlessly, and earnestly. When we are diligent in our desire to please God such diligence leaves little time for dangerous imagination, which can exalt itself above the knowledge of God. Hence, our diligence will cause us to prayerfully wait on God rather than seek a quick-fix for our dilemmas or run at the first sign of trouble.

Defeat the Hazards of Worry

HOW MANY AREAS of our past are marred with poor decisions that have been presumptuously acted upon simply because we lacked the faith and trust to patiently wait on God? As trite as it may sound, *'wait'* is not a dirty, four-letter word. But it appears to have become so for many of today's believers. People today change churches like they change their clothes. Everyone refers to 'my' ministry when talking about their spiritual ambitions; and no one seem to fear saying, "the Lord said," speaking visions out of their own hearts and not from the mouth of God! (*ref.* Jeremiah 23:16) For where does this boldness come? Is it not presumptuousness and the worry of one's self-image? David even asked God to deliver him from presumptuous sins (*ref.* Psalm 19:13).

Presumptuous sin reflects rebellion, which seeks to force God to accept our choices even if it's against His Word. In other words, we place His label on a product He did not produce and presume it will give the same results after it's sold! How generic! Remember, His will is revealed in His Word, and so often people who are operating under a sinful presumptuous spirit, reject the sound counsel of God's word when their minds are made up to do their own thing. There is a passage in Proverbs (21:5), which says, ***"The thoughts of the diligent tend only to be plenteousness; but of every one that is hasty only want."*** This powerful little proverb can help defeat the hazards of worry which can dangerously manifest themselves in our behavior. This happens because we have to redo things which were not initially done according to God's will. This leads to ill-advised, hasty actions which only satisfies us for the moment, but will ultimately leaves us wanting.

No Time To Redo

The mind-set of the trusting child of God produces divine abundance. Why? Because his decisions and actions are not motivated by the flesh, but are ordered by the Lord. When we move outside of the will of God we position ourselves to have to redo those things, which could have originally been done according to God's plan. So much time is wasted when we have to repeat a step that could have been prayerfully executed. It is not my intent to repeat myself but to drive home a thought I've learned the hard way. In some circumstances it's not that the impending action is wrong or even sinful, but that the timing of it or the season matters greatly when seeking God's will. Time is so very precious and must be used wisely. Although *time* is not *eternity*, what is done in time, however, can have eternal implications.

Since God holds both time and eternity in His hands it's best to wait on Him. Contrary to what you may think, 'wait' is not designed to simply keep you on ice. When the instructions to wait have come from God there is never any time lost, no matter how long it takes. Remember that God is in control of time. He's the God who, in hearkening to the voice of a mere man caused the sun and the moon to stand still at the word of Joshua. (*ref.* Joshua 10:12)

Impulsiveness A Tool of the Will

MOST IMPULSIVENESS is motivated by selfish or soulish thoughts. Let me take a moment to talk about our soulish realm verses our spirit-man. There is a battle going on within us. It's the battle of the soul and the spirit. Once our spirit has been regenerated by the Holy Spirit, we then engage in the process of holiness and the subduing of our will. This is not a simple process because our soulish-will doesn't want to submit to the Spirit of God, which is now governing our spirit. Remember, our will gained its control at the fall of Adam and had its way from then until Pentecost. So while our spirits are hearing the Word of God instructing us on how to wait on Him, our wills are rationalizing in our minds what is really in our own best interest; even if it is contrary to what God has said. Remember the flesh is enmity against the laws of God.

Whenever we attempt to rationalize our way into disobedience, we must collect data or thoughts which make sense to our senses. Worry aids in this process by reminding us of what we see, or in other words, how things *look*! Worry helps process the information or reports we've heard. It justifies the anxious emotions we feel! It is not designed to inspire our spirit toward faith! It's designed to be a tool of the will in an effort to decide what is best for us. If we don't master worry and bring it captive, we will find ourselves moving when God says, *"Stand still!"* We must face the fact that this type of disobedience is disrespectful and shows an irreverence toward God.

Driven to Do Something

SOMETIMES WE THINK of ourselves in light of what others have, or in terms of what we are missing. There are even thoughts in our minds of how we look to others or who we're impressing. This is prevalent because we live in a day when people are quick to evaluate others based on what they possess. The Madison-Avenue, high profile image common to the world of advertising has sharpen the public relation's image of the contemporary church. The spirit of excellence demands that we make our best presentation. But many have taken this obsession with image to the extreme. The world calls it, "keeping up with the Joneses." If these thoughts aren't brought under discipline, we will act out of carnal motivation believing we're doing something godly. Impulsive actions have deferred many goals because people felt they *had* to do something. Often these impulsive actions are our way of trying to *prove* to others God is with us too! In other words, if God doesn't move then I will! How disrespectful!

This thinking has too often pervaded such areas of our lives as intimate relationships, career decisions, and even ministry choices. In these times many have taken an "in your face" approach towards dealing with God, spawned from the fret of impending missed-opportunities. Consequently, they approach issues as though they must take matters into their own hands lest life pass them by. Some even feel as though God's standards are keeping them from being happy or reaching a level of achievement. Rather than being godly and content, many are looking at others to define how they are and what they should be doing. This is especially dangerous when we look to the world and its system to define satisfaction, success, happiness and prosperity. Paul, however, explains for us that ***"Godliness with contentment is great gain..."*** (*ref.* I Timothy 6:6) Paul said, he had learned in whatsoever state he was in therewith to be content. (*ref.* Philippians 4:11)

Influence Which Opens Doors

NO ONE ENJOYS A SLACKER not even God, but many people actually worry about their image as a go-getter or an achievers, thinking that if they do something or obtain more, it will gain for them acceptance and approval. If someone doesn't like you as you are, you can never do enough to please them. Whatever rules they have for inclusion into their world will constantly change when it comes to you. So relax! Stop worrying! There are some parties you are not going to be invited to. But, life goes on! It really doesn't matter. A closer look will reveal God is the One who won't allow you to fit into some circles of influence. He alone wants to be the Influence, which opens your doors. As a result of some people's worrying about validation or approval years have been wasted not pleasing the One who loves them and is ordering their steps. Sadly, many don't have much to show for their years of existence due to poor, hasty decisions which have consistently produced lack and left them wanting. The writer of Hebrews says, ***"Let our conversation be without covetousness; and be content with such things as ye have: for he hath said, I will never leave thee, nor forsake thee."*** (*ref.* Hebrews 13:6).

I once heard someone say something that stuck with me: "You wouldn't care what people think of you, if you only knew how seldom they do." Don't worry about things that really aren't important, let alone things that are. For the important things, seek God for wisdom to handle it. Life is too short and eternity is too long to be wrong. Live your life for God, service to other and your time to those who matter most.

Remember the passage, which says ***"For I know the thoughts and plans that I have for you, says the Lord, thoughts and plans for welfare and peace, and not for evil to give you hope in your final outcome."*** (*ref.* Jeremiah 29:11 AMP) Having this knowledge ends the compulsions that are stimulated by poor and unbiblical decisions. It will do wonders in creating or re-establishing an intimate relationship with the Lord that will ultimately produce reverence and honor, not consumed by man's opinions. God has a plan, and in the final outcome there is hope! Just knowing your life and times are in His hands will cause your life to be more focused and productive.

Results of Vision, Motives and Faith

IT IS TIME for us to forget about all of the little issues that seem to cloud our minds and keep us from realizing our dreams and potential. We have the God-given ability to make a difference in our communities and even the world. Change will never be affected if we don't learn how to handle our worries and stop allowing worry to handle us. Proverbs 16:3 says, ***"Commit thy works unto the Lord, and thy thoughts shall be established."*** In this passage the word *"commit"* means to transfer a burden from your shoulders to that of One who is stronger and better able to bear it. The Lord had given me this powerful passage while worrying about whether our ministry would be able to open a private, Christian school. The enormity of the endeavor had me apprehensive.

I knew the Lord had directed me to address the lack of quality education for our children, but our ministry was young and we were considering not only the physical challenges of housing a school, but salaries and the development of a full-time staff as well.

Nonetheless, God began to deal with me about motives, why we do the things we do. Once being fully convinced that our efforts had nothing to do with the applause of men we took a worry-free approach to executing the vision. However, in a board meeting from which I was absent the board continued discussions about the challenges of providing security for the personnel. They were concerned about the principal who would be leaving a job of benefits. I must admit I was concerned also, but I knew God had instructed us to open this school. Now began the true test of faith.

Every Vision Must Have Water -Walkers

I WENT BACK to the next board meeting and told the them, "I still believe we could do it...." With the new principal now standing in faith with me I admonished them that with any great challenge, risks must be taken. I explained that it was a lot like the disciples in the boat telling Peter why he couldn't walk on the water. The idea of walking on water is great but it takes enormous faith in God to even fathom the very thought. Anything of greatness will cost you something!

After one of the longest meetings we ever had, we saw things turn around before our eyes. We all began to see our faith being stretched to accomplish the impossible. Hearing all of the legitimate concerns and separating them from our worries, we not only left the meeting with a unanimous decision to open that September, but we also agreed to take a worry-free approach towards the other challenges facing us. Each board member realized there would be a personal cost and sacrifice they would incur. In other words this endeavor would require us all leaving the boat and walking on water, though some may walk further than others. As a result we saw the various sacrifices of the board members, each knowing that if God said it, He is more than able to bring it to pass! By the time we concluded the meeting, we had even raised a seed offering as a demonstration of our faith. To date, the Grace Christian Preparatory Academy has been opened with an increase in staff, grade levels added and a waiting list for enrollment.

In short, worry will keep you at the discussion-table and cause you to miss your window of opportunity. It is God who is working within us both the *will* and the *do* of His good pleasure (*ref.* Philippians 2:13), therefore we must move without fear when He says *"Move!"* Stand still without pressure when He says *"Wait!"* For to do otherwise, no matter how justifiable, is irreverent.

7

END THE LEPROSY

"Leprosy like cancer doesn't care that you are dying in its attempt to thrive. It has no concern about what its presence has done to your quality of life. It must survive at any cost, even if you must die."

IT IS AMAZING how we can maintain a particular mind-set for so long that we begin to believe that our way of thinking is the *only* way to think. Recently the Lord spoke to me concerning my enemy. A large majority of people view the enemy's attacks as primarily external in it's impact. Most see the enemy as something or someone working against them, mainly as an external adversary. I must confess that initially this had been my primary school of thought.

While for the most part this is true, recently God let me know we needed to adjust our opinion in this area. Often we can think we're okay, but it's not until after God uses the magnifying glass of His Word to show us ourselves that we are truly made right in a particular area. I was made to clearly see that our real enemies are *internal*. This realization is much more than the old adage, which says, "You are your own worst enemy!"

Proverbs 24:17-18 showed me the area of growth I needed in order for Him to protect me from my enemy. As I read the following passage which says, ***"Rejoice not when thine enemy falleth, and let not thine heart be glad when he stumbleth: Lest the Lord see it, and it displease Him, and He turn away His wrath from him…"*** The Lord dealt with me about the anxiety of vengeance. Vengeance is the desire for retribution against your enemy. The anxiety of vengeance occurs when it appears your offender will not receive his just recompense or that you will not have the luxury of witnessing it.

As I look back now I realize God was really preparing me to minister to others in this area. You would be surprised at the countless number of individuals who worry about offenses committed against them. Much has been written about this subject, yet many still find it difficult to release offensive issues into the hands of the Lord and live worry-free. Asaph, the levitical psalmist and songwriter of David's day wrote, ***"My feet were almost gone; my steps had well nigh slipped. For I was envious at the foolish when I saw the prosperity of the wicked."*** (*ref.* Psalm 73:2-3)

Whose Got Your Tongue

DAVID, THE AUTHOR of Psalms 37, provides for us an assurance that there is a blessing in godly living. He establishes that any prosperity of the wicked is short-lived and insecure. This prosperity should not be considered just in terms of the materialistic things of life. Prosperity can be the advancement of an individual or his personal accomplishments. There are stages in life where the voice of your enemy seems to prosper. There are times when the opinions of others are advancing.

And it's a very sad fact of "church" life that people are so prone to believe what they hear. In fact we are admonished that the only time hearing is more important then seeing is in matters of faith. (*ref.* Saint John 7:24, 51)

During those obscure periods of vast ridicule God deliberately has you in a place where He won't allow you to advance your cause. Hence you are forced to hold your peace. In this Psalm, David gives us some instructions directed towards man's propensity to worry about what he sees. David is so emphatic that he commands us in the very first verse: ***"Fret not thyself because of evildoers, neither be thou envious..."*** (*ref.* Psalm 37:1) I believe he begins with this commandment because it is hard to obey the other commandments until you have mastered your own feelings and emotions. He clearly recognizes the activity of the evildoer as something, which must be dealt with, because on two other occasions he says, ***"fret not..."*** verses 7 & 8: ***"fret not thyself because of him who prospereth in his way" and "fret not thyself in any wise to do evil."***

I found it interesting to know that to fret is 'to severely worry' or 'to become troubled by'; also it is 'to torment oneself.' This is biblical proof that worry can have a chronic affect on an individual. It was not until I discovered how the Scripture uses the word "fret" that I realized how serious the matter really was. This is when I began to reconsider the *internal enemy* versus the *external adversary*. The word fret or fretting means 'to gnaw or eat away at' or 'to corrode'. In the Old Testament's description of the dreadful disease called leprosy, a particular form of leprosy was called a "fretting leprosy". It was singled out because of its distinctive hidden nature and its ability to eat away at whatever it came in contact. This disease was so potent that, even when hidden, its effects could be seen rotting the clothing of its victim, hence their garments would have to be burned.

When Evergreens Go Dry

THE HOLY SPIRIT is sending this rhema word to perform a priestly cleansing in many of the lives of those who are reading this book. You may be about to perish because you have questions about how someone whose venomous touch, which has been the caused you much grief, broken relationships and pain, could seemingly continue to prosper. David described it well in Psalm 37:35, ***"I have seen the wicked in great power, and spreading himself like a green bay tree."*** A green bay tree is most familiar when described as an evergreen tree, a tree that is green all year round. I understand that even though you know you're not perfect you can't help wondering how you can do good and still have to struggle, while others can obviously do wrong or mishandle the righteous and still seem to exist with prosperity. My friends, this kind of mental activity will disturb your mind if you don't know the Word of God and God's justice. You must know God has a *perfect will* for those with a *perfect heart.* Yes your heart can be perfect even if you're not. And God is a God who honors motives.

The message is that the wicked may be prospering or appearing to do so, but it's only for a season. Even the green bay tree David described had an end. According to verse 36 David says, ***"Yet he passed away, and lo, he was not: yea I sought him, but he could not be found."*** Relax, your enemy is not the issue. God is more concerned with you. The first thing you must do in order for your life to prosper is to take your eyes off of the enemy and stop worrying about how they are thriving. If you aren't careful this type of worry can lead to a disease in *your* spirit! Before you know it, your spirit and attitude will become corroded like a *"fretting leprosy."* Once you allow this to happen you will have no one to blame but yourself.

Your offense is yours as long as you choose to possess it. You don't have to own the hurts. It is not *"your pain"* or *"your hurt."* Start by changing your language! Remember, it's only *yours* if you choose to *own it.* I discovered offenses only hurt as long as you are *offended.* Once you come to the realization (like Joseph), ***"they meant it for evil but God meant it for good..."*** (*ref.* Genesis 50:20) you can release yourself from the spirit of offense. Hurts can lead to worry, worries to fretting, fretting to bitterness and the Bible says the ***root of bitterness troubles you*!** (*ref.* Hebrews 12:15) To offend is to make 'to stumble.' Its meaning is derived from the Greek word *'skandalon'*, meaning to *bait, trap,* and *snare* or to *dig*. This is where we derive our English word 'scandal'. There are some situations where the individual who offends may actually feel he has done God a service by his actions of creating or highlighting an offense. But people who think this way should remember how God used Babylon to chasten Israel, but He then judged Babylon for allowing themselves to be used against His people!

Nevertheless, in order to be offended, you must choose to be so. In other words, *offense is a matter of choice.* You can either focus on the offense and worry about vengeance or you can concentrate on your relationship with God and trust His *defense.* Your ownership of the offense will, in time, corrode your spirit and trouble you. Others externally can offend but internally only *you* can fret *yourself* over the offense. By doing so, you will become a victim of a fretting leprosy with symptoms of anger, bitterness, mistrust, apprehension and fear. And all of this can even lead to physical and mental illness.

It's clear that David's instructions are, simply, "Do not allow yourself to be vexed!"

Guess Who Gets The Last Laugh

ONE WAY TO UNDERSTAND the plight of the wicked is to read the Psalms and the Proverbs to see their ultimate end. Proverbs 24:19, 20 says ***"Fret not thyself because of evil men, neither be thou envious at the wicked: for there shall be no reward to the evil man; the candle of the wicked shall be put out."*** You are cautioned not to take up his ways. No matter what the world says, you can't fight fire with fire. As a child of God, you simply have to wait for the candle of the wicked to be put out. I must admonish you that you also can't rejoice at the fall of the wicked, when it does come. (*ref.* Proverbs 24:17-18) God is saying to you, ***"don't you laugh when they fall, or then I'll become angry with you."*** The fall of the wicked may be a laughing matter but, God says, He'll do the laughing for you (*ref.* Psalm 37:13): ***"The Lord shall laugh at him: for he seeth that his day is coming."***

Don't Be Bitter, Be Better

THEN WHAT'S a person to do? Here are the rest of your divine instructions. Five of the seven commandments found in Psalm 37 relate to the Lord. They involve an individual's interaction with Him. We are told to ***"trust, delight, commit, rest in and wait on the Lord".*** The other two commandments refer to our emotions and us. God assumes the majority of the responsibility, thereby allowing us the joy of His companionship. We are told to ***"fret not"*** and ***"cease from anger,"*** if we want to see the Lord's hand at work on our behalf. If we do not master our two mandated responsibilities we will never experience the peace that comes through the other five admonishments.

We simply cannot allow the subtlety of worry over unresolved issues or hurts to fester in our spirits, ***"lest any root of bitterness springing up troubles you and thereby many be defiled."*** (*ref.* Hebrews 12:15) The results can be devastating because they can produce a fretting disease that, like cancer, can eat away at all the good in its selfish effort to survive. But leprosy, unlike cancer, defiles not only the person with the disease, but all who come in contact with him. Hence, bitterness is an infectious disease!

Leprosy doesn't care that you are dying in its attempt to thrive. It has no concern about what its presence has done to your quality of life. It must survive at any cost, even if you must die. It is the same with some people who have disappointments, and the pain they will not release. Many people don't realize that by holding on to these things they are providing an incubation chamber for a disease which, if allowed to grow, will ultimately destroy them. It is better that *you* live and allow some issues to die. Release them and let them go. Better still, release yourself!

One of the smallest and simplest words in our language can be the most difficult to perform. It's the word, *"let"*, which among its various definitions means to "allow, permit, release, give over to" or "to surrender by hand". Hence, when the scriptures say, "*let*" it places us in control of what the Holy Spirit is asking of us. There are many examples throughout the Scriptures, but here's one example, which provides a cure for any fretting leprosy, ***"LET all bitterness and wrath, and anger, evil speaking, be put away from you with all malice: And BE ye kind one to another, tender hearted, forgiving one another, even as God for Christ's sake hath forgiven you."*** (*ref.* Ephesians 4:31-32) The word 'be' is another one of those tiny word with enormous weight of responsibility when utter by the voice of God. Let God raise up friends, establish relationships, create new opportunities for you and prosper you in due season. He will do it all according to His timing and wisdom if you don't fret and if you faint not. You do have the power to stand; and ***"having done all to stand"*** simply, ***"Stand!"*** The more you allow yourself to be healed of past hurts and pains the more strength you will receive as you continue to stand.

Knowing you have God's favor will give you the release you need from some and the power to be to others what you are ordained to be. There is a cure for the fretting leprosy cause by worries associated with hurts and not allowing oneself to forgive. Once you let go, your healing will begin. Therefore, LET go and LIVE by destroying the things which seek to destroy you.

8

AN ENEMY OF WORSHIP

"God can't reveal anything to your mind if your mind is cluttered with meaningless thoughts... Worship prepares your mind and spirit to be the canvas by which the Holy Spirit can paint the knowledge of God and His perfect will."

THE ENEMY KNOWS you cannot be effective as a servant of the Lord as long as your mind is constrained. Accordingly, we cannot praise God or give Him true worship as long as we are perplexed. Worship can only be accomplished in the spirit of man. So many believers have not experienced true worship because their spirits are not truly free due to needless anxiety. The first thing we must do to free ourselves from this tool of the enemy is to live our lives according to biblical principles. The Word contains answers that address all the "issues of life." The Book of Proverbs is an unmatched source for practical life-guidance and a wonderful aide in freeing one's spirit in times of concern and trouble. The assurance given in the basic areas of life provides tools for productive and abundant living. I've discovered a solace I can't explain when pondering the outcome of situations unknown. I've discovered verses which have become practical antidotes for survival. Often, I must stop reading and immediately begin worshiping God at the very thought that He has so readily provided a way of escape for me through the mediation of His Word. My friend, by truly making Christ Lord over every dimension of our lives we begin to experience "worry-free" living which is part of the abundant life promised to us. And this life free of anxiety can be experienced even in the most severe storm.

If we are going to live the life of Christ we must arrive at the place where, short of constructive and productive concerns, we learn to function absolutely worry-free. It is true that life comes with its own collection of challenges and frustrations. But, we must move into that sphere that Paul talked about, the state of being "*careful for nothing.*" Don't simply thank God *for* some things but learn to thank Him *in* all things. This is when worship begins. Remember that everyday you wake up you awaken to new mercies. Don't be dismayed by the cares of life or the attacks of the enemy. Use those attacks as measuring rods of your maturity in God and learn to benefit from them.

A Strange Reason To Glory

SATAN WILL ONLY attack you as you continue to triumph from one circumstance to another. Even though you may or may not know the specifics of your outcome God uses these assaults to develop a confident maturity in you. When you trust Him you will continue to have an assurance even when circumstances befall you, that it will all work out for your good. Remember what Paul said, ***"...We glory in tribulations..."*** (*ref.* Romans 5:3), talking about worry-free living,

Paul had actually mastered it so well that his attacks became reason for him to glory. In fact he even said he was ***"exceedingly joyful in all (his) tribulation,"*** and in another place he said *"**Therefore... I take pleasure in infirmities, reproaches, necessities, persecutions, and in distresses for Christ's sake: for when I am weak, then am I strong.**"* (*ref.* 2 Corinthians 12:10) Many of these encouraging words were written while Paul was in a dark,dirty, smelly prison.

Is there something mentally wrong with Paul's thinking or has he unearthed the secret to worry-free, Christ-centered living? What Paul realizes is that it's all working for his good. ***"...Knowing that tribulations worketh patience, and patience experience, and experience hope and hope maketh not ashamed."*** In other words, everything is working together and in the end you won't be disappointed. ***"Trust in the Lord with all thine heart; and lean not unto thine own understanding. In all thy ways acknowledge Him and He shall direct thy paths."*** (*ref.* Proverbs 3:4-5) These passages are able to sustain you when you are prone to worry.

Your Mind, An Awesome Thing to Waste

BEFORE OUR SPIRITS can worship we must be free in our minds. Remember the passage where Paul said, ***"with my mind I serve the Lord..."*** He would not have been able to do this except by taking control of his thoughts and making them subject to the law of God. Take note of Paul's letter to the Philippians. Throughout this epistle Paul continues to mention the mind or things associated with ones thinking. Note the impact of the mind on Christian behavior and performance:

- In Philippians 1:3-4, Paul illustrates that joyful

memories produces grateful hearts;

- In verse 27 the people are admonished that singleness of mind will keep them "striving together for the faith."

- It is in chapter 2 that Paul assures them that within their conflict as with his, they can discover the blessings of consolation, comfort, communion, and compassion. He again charges them to be of the same mind.

- In verses 5-8 he speaks of having a humble mind, which was like the mind of Christ and that this mind should be in you which was also in Christ.

- By verses 13 and 14, Paul talks about the process of mental elimination, by forgetting past things and pressing forward.

- Therefore, by the time he comes to the final chapter 4, he can say to the church to be careful for nothing, which means be anxious for nothing.

- By verse 8 Paul is telling us how to occupy our thinking and what types of things we should be thinking.

Paul has discovered this tremendous use of the mind for spiritual living and godly pursuit. He shows us how the mind is an essential yet wonderful tool in one's walk with God. He further affirms that this mental tool should not be wasted! He even speaks of the war between the law of his members and the law of his mind. (*ref.* Romans 7:23) Then Paul further speaks of the carnal mind being an enemy of God, producing death. But the spiritual mind produces life and peace. (*ref.* Romans 8:5-7) Can you now see why Paul affirms in Romans

7:25 that *"with the mind we serve the law of God?"* Again, without proper thinking we can't accomplish godly living. And those who would be perfect should have the same mind. God's Word is His law.

Therefore, we must apply His Word to those thoughts which would otherwise captivate us. The consistent application of God's Word will cause the mind to change, thereby becoming the mind of Christ. This is the renewed mind Paul talks about, which will ultimately transform us. (*ref.* Romans 12:2)

Don't Lose Sight of the Bigger Picture

A STRONG COMPONENT of worry is unpleasant thoughts. These thoughts and images can be uncontrollable at times. Nearly all worry occurs by imagining thoughts of "what-ifs!" We worry about things that rarely happen the way we imagine they will, if at all. Even if the end results are as bad as we'd imagined what good can really come from worrying? The worry will cause us to lose sight of the bigger picture: Our calling and purpose.

Worry is like people who arrive at the movies after the picture has already begun. Just as the good scenes are showing or when the protagonist's problems are finally being explained, worry like some people, will stroll right in front of the camera, successfully magnifying its shadow onto the screen. Remember, this shadow is not a part of the picture, it simply occupies a presence on the screen and obstructs your view while the movie is playing. Every time a scene comes which you are straining to see (understand), worry stands up and cast its shadow over our thinking!

There is one more thing you must remember about this movie-theatre scenario. The only way the divine picture can be seen is that God uses the faith of His Word as film, the very material the story is etched on. But film can't be completely understood or seen until the Light passes through it. Jesus Christ *is* that light, and His will is the magnifying glass. The only way worry's images can be seen at all is because it is *in front* of the Light. And any thing that we allow to stand in front of God's Word is *not* of God. Therefore, we must be aggressive in dealing with negative images on the screens of our minds lest such obtrusive thoughts continue to plague us throughout life. Paul tells us to pull and cast down everything which ***exalts itself above the knowledge of God!*** (*ref.* 2 Corinthians 10:5) Moreover, God knew all the problems you would encounter when he made the choice of you as His servant. So enjoy the picture, no matter how it looks! It gets better the closer you get to the end!

I'm sure Paul pondered the purpose of his beatings and imprisonments, but look how deprived we would be today had Paul simply sat around his jail cell and worried over the the *"why"* of his situation--feeling sorry for himself. Paul wrote two-thirds of the New Testament, much of which was written while in prison. This is largely due to the fact that he went into the prison with a *mind* to serve God in whatever state he found himself. Even though Paul may have been talking to the Corinthians, God had us in mind when Paul wrote: ***"For out of much affliction and anguish of heart I wrote unto you with many tears; not that you should be grieved, but that ye might know the love which I have more abundantly unto you."*** (*ref.* 2 Corinthians 2:4)

Throughout Paul's numerous writings he managed to warn us against worrying saying we should continue the task of ***"casting down imaginations."*** (*ref.* 2 Corinthians 10:5) The "s" on the end of "imagination" lets us know there are various types of *imaginations*. Worry produces mental visions, therefore it qualifies as an imagination. Hence, it should be thrown down! Moreover, he writes that not only should we pull down strongholds and cast down imaginations, but ***"every high thing that exalteth itself against the knowledge of God, bringing into captivity every thought to the obedience of Christ."*** Let's face it, it's hard to be obedient to God when your thoughts of "What if?", "Why me?", and "When will I?" are dominating your mind. These questions of worry will presents reasons why you can't when God says, "YOU CAN."

Worry offers alternatives that are contradictory to the challenges of your faith. The problem we have in the house of God is that we have too many people who are free in their souls (being saved) but are bound in their minds. Paul says there's only one way to deal with this, "catch it, pull it down and destroy it." Don't take worry for granted it's a stronghold with which one must confront. Before this can be achieved, one must master control of those thoughts.

Relationship Produces Genuine Worship

HENCE, ONE OF the greatest hindrances to worship is worry. You see worship is the affirming of God's character and nature. We praise Him for what He has done, but we worship Him for who He is. Worship also denotes relationship. When we worship, we must move beyond the *sense* realm and adore God for who He is based upon our knowledge of Him. This knowledge only comes through a relationship. For example, when I worship God as a healer, deliverer, and all-sufficient God, I'm left to experience a negative situation which contradicts my worship. That becomes a perfect time for the enemy to attack me mentally. He brings thoughts that invade my worship. But the beautiful thing about worship is that it doesn't just involve my mind or will, but it is primarily reliant upon my spirit. Jesus said, we must worship God in spirit and in truth. Therefore, no matter what comes nigh me, through my spirit I am able to rise above it when I worship.

Remember when the Apostle John who was exiled to a place called Patmos, a rocky island in the midst of the Mediterranean? John was placed there, not because of any wrong that he had done, but because of preaching the ***"... word of God, and for the testimony of Jesus Christ"*** (*ref.* Revelation 1:9). Look at what John did. Although he was in a foreign, deserted and potentially dangerous place filled with the distracting sounds of raving beasts and the blackness of a thousand nights he yet sought to have fellowship with God. John said, ***"I was in the Spirit on the Lord's day... "*** (*ref.* verse 10). As John worshiped in the human spirit, the Spirit *of God* lifted him and took him into the heavenlies. As a result of seeking to worship God in the Spirit, despite his current conditions, God was able to trust John with revelations.

God can't reveal anything to your mind if it's cluttered with meaningless thoughts that have nothing to do with divine possibility. Worship prepares your mind and spirit to be the canvas on which the Holy Spirit paints the knowledge of God and His perfect will. Worry will only hinder and prevent this process, but worship will bring divine revelation and peaceful understanding. Though John's physical man was confined to a wilderness, his spirit-man could not be put into confinement because it was in the throne-room of God!

When your adversaries create circumstances hoping to confine and control you don't stop worshipping! Though your exile can be arranged and even carried out, as long as you know how to worship God in Spirit and in truth, you will never, ever be a victim of man's devices!

Once we have learned to manage our worries we will have some additional time on our hands. Yes, time for doing something for Christ, but also for creative thinking as well. Releasing worry also releases more mental and emotional space. If you wonder what to do with all that extra time consider our Philippians scripture in verse 8 of the 4th chapter, *"Whatsoever things are true, honest, just, pure, and of good report; if there be any virtue, if there be any praise, "think on these things."* Virtuous thoughts clear the mind for creative thinking, productivity and divine possibilities!

9

CONCERNED NOT CAREFUL

"... When we pray, we cannot allow worry to cross over into our supplication because, once it does, the prayer becomes solicitous. Those who solicit believe their agenda is more important than yours."

THE PREVALENCE of worry is rooted in the fact that so many people worry about common things. Many Christians still have not realized that concerns for life's basic necessities should not plague them so intensely. Show me a believer who has struggles in these basic necessities and I'll show you evidence of improper management, disobedience in giving, and worse still, carnal thinking. For example, it's amazing how many professing Christians claim to have a relationship with the Lord yet complain about their financial struggles. They maintain that their struggle is so severe that they're unable to afford tithing. They don't understand that these problems exist in the first place because they're not in covenant with God in areas of giving.

However, there are some tithers that, though they are experiencing some blessings, don't receive all they are promised due to improper management. Regardless of which category one falls within, once worry is added you have an equation for not only a life lived below God's promised standards, but also one filled with mental anguish. Hence, the prevailing challenge to all believers is to "*... seek ye first the kingdom of God, and His righteousness; and all these things shall be added unto you.*" (*ref.* Saint Matthew. 6:33) In this familiar passage Jesus admonishes us of the proper thinking for the child of God. God always requires the *first* of whatever we have or do.

In My Father's House

EVEN IN THE AREA of seeking our own welfare, we should not allow it to take precedence over our spiritual well being. He says that "these things", referring to basic necessities of life, are a given. Obviously, they are a part of the "children's bread"-- those things God will provide for us simply because we are His children. Provisional bread reserved for the children of the Father is not something which is sought or begged for, it is in every house where God is the Father.

Here's a familiar illustration of what I mean. I'm a father and one of my major concerns is for my daughter's welfare. It was important that she had shelter, food, and clothing, simply because she's my child. These things have nothing to do with preferences, rewards and other benevolent amenities. Although this was a greater concern when she was a minor than now, the principle still remains true. As long as she lives in my house, she will never beg for bread.

When we consider its ramifications we realize that this concept of provisions in the house is so awesome! Even the prodigal son understood that, although he had disappointed his father and was not sure of what to expect upon his return home, he knew even the hired servants had provisions simply because they too were in the house. In the spiritual realm, our maturity is reflective of our obedience. Though we continue to be His children, God expects us to adhere to His Word. This adherence assures us of His continuous provisions above and beyond anything we could ask or think.

As a good father, I should ensure that my daughter's welfare does not become a source of worry for her. Even as she's matured into adulthood she should realize that a loving father (not to mention, an awesome mother) provided the tools for successful living! Saint Luke 11:13 states, ***"If our earthly fathers know how to provide for their children how much more will God (our Heavenly Father) provide good gifts if we ask Him"*** (--MONT). Unfortunately, for many Christians, worry finds its roots in these basic necessities of life. If we are going to have a wholesome relationship with the Father it must begin with the basics. These basic necessities should never be an issue with the child of God. Our testimonies shouldn't be about God's provision of the basics. It would sound ridiculous hearing your children testifying about food, clothing and raiment.

Even now, I contend that until I give my adult daughter into the hands of a man who can provide for her in these and greater areas I'm still actively involved in her temporal welfare and preparation for life.

There are major issues and crises of life relevant to health and family, which may justifiably cause us concern. The operative word to consider is *"concern"*. The Scriptures provide rich examples of how God intervenes in the issues and concerns of His people. Yet the same Scripture clearly establishes for us a marked difference between having *concerns* and being *careful* or *anxious*. Even in our concerns, we must exercise our faith and belief that God is still able to perform what is best for us.

This point may not be very clear for some because of the

manner in which we commonly use the word *"careful."* When we use certain words in our English language we sometimes lose the true meaning of the word, moreover, its biblical connotation is rarely ever realized at face value. The word *"careful"* is a good example. Often when we refer to being *careful* we are admonishing someone to be *cautious*. While there may be some overlapping in meaning, when the Bible speaks of ***"being careful for nothing..."*** it means *"do not be anxious or solicitous."* (*ref.* Philippians 4:6) The main ingredient of anxiety or solicitude is fear.

Don't Even Think About It

ACCORDINGLY, when your concerns about anything begin to manifest feelings of fear or apprehension they are no longer mere concerns but worries, or what the Bible calls ***"being careful"***, or "full of care." Consider also that in the Greek the word also means, *"merman"*, meaning, *"to take thought."* And when you worry, you literally *take thought away* from the things you should be giving thought to.

This is why we cannot allow worry to cross over into our supplication when we pray. Once it does, the prayer becomes solicitous. It's easy for us to know when this happens because we start pleading instead of praying, and there is absolutely nothing gracious about solicitation. In fact it can be a debasing experience. There's something else I discovered about solicitation. Those who solicit believe *their* agenda is more important than *yours*. This is why David affirms that solicitation is not a part of the lifestyle of the righteous. He asserts, ***"I have been young, and now am old; yet have I not seen the righteous forsaken nor his seed begging bread."*** (*ref.* Psalms 37:25) God doesn't want to hear His children begging Him in their prayers. That's demeaning to Him as a Father and, I am sure, embarrassing, if overheard by another believer or non-believer.

If you were in public and observed a child desperately begging and pleading with his father for something to eat, you would call the local child protective services agency. Yet there are times when a child may beg, not out of sincere need or for anything of real value and a true father will have to make a decision to deny that child his request. In that situation, the father recognizes that what his child really needs is the maturation that will be developed during this process of denial. He knows by doing this that child will eventually learn to make better decisions for himself.

Denial is as much a part of parenting as giving. When we are denied anything by God we should never beg Him as if He is withholding something from us. God is not an abusive father, but that doesn't mean He will give us everything we want simply because we ask. There are times when we must petition Him. Hence, prayer can be supplication (to ask or entreat humbly and earnestly) but it should never be solicitation. It is the presence or absence of relationship and knowledge which determines whether we supplicate or solicit.

How Do You Call Heaven

HAVE YOU EVER received a phone call from a telephone solicitor? They seem to call at a time when you're engaged in activity that is important to you. Once they get you on the phone, it may take everything short of rudeness to get them off the telephone. Why? Because whatever they're selling, their quota, or their commission is more important to them than your time or agenda. Granted, I'm only talking about the inconsiderate ones. There are some who are successful and for good reason. In my scenario there is a secret to supplication which can avoid the threat of solicitation. When you pray, never call heaven as if your needs or desires are the only thing that's important to God. Supplication will cause you to struggle with your own will until *God's* agenda becomes the only thing that matters. Which of the two have you been doing in your prayer time? If you've been soliciting, chances are your worry habit is affecting your relationship with and knowledge of God! Hence, your prayers are going unanswered.

When we understand worry in its proper context, the charge to, ***"be careful for nothing,"*** will cause us to look at other passages in the Scriptures differently when we see the word "careful." In Philippians 4:6, Paul is saying something more than not to be anxious, he is actually telling us not to tolerate anxiety or worry because it will injure the soul. God alone can help you and He will if you pray about everything, doubt Him for nothing, and give thanks in everything. Jesus puts it this way, ***"Take therefore no thought for the morrow: for the morrow shall take thought for the things of itself. Sufficient unto the day is the evil thereof."*** (*ref.* Saint Matthew 6:34) He's admonishing us to take no anxious, perplexing or worrying thought.

Look at it this way, the presence of control in our lives tends to make us secure and thus worry-free. It is only when control is threatened or things appear out of our control that worry seems to find a safe haven in our minds. For the child of God there is added security in life because when we feel that things are out of control there is still no need for us to lose control. Why? God is in control and the mere thought of this reality should bring us immediate peace and absolute calm. Our relationship with God becomes a trade-off when we surrender our limited in securities and accept His boundless securities. This boundless security is only encountered through trusting Him.

Vision Beyond The Visible

THE MOST PERFECT illustration of worry-free living is the example Jesus provided when He used *"the birds to illustrate freedom from anxiety, the lilies to illustrate freedom from status seeking, and the grass...to illustrate our need to assess priorities."*[5] Having addressed the subject of anxiety in our earlier chapters we must give some attention to status-seeking and the need to assess priorities if we are going to completely address worry-free living. According to Jeremiah 17:8 ***"The man who trusts in the Lord shall not worry in the years of drought and will not stop bearing fruit..."*** (-MONT). In fact, not only are the barren instructed not to worry, they are admonished to sing, ***"...For more are the children of the desolate than the children of the married wife."*** (*ref.* Isaiah 54:1).

Pastors take note of what I found as an answer to ministry expansion in the midst of lack. The writer goes on to say,

> ***"...Enlarge the place of thy tent, and let them stretch forth the curtains of thine habitations: spare not, lengthen thy cords, and strengthen thy stakes; For thou shalt break forth on the right hand and on the left... Fear not; for thou shalt not be ashamed: neither be thou confounded; for thou shalt not be put to shame... For thy Maker is thine husband; the Lord of host is His name; and thy Redeemer the Holy One of Israel; the God of the whole earth shall He be called. No weapon that is formed against thee shall prosper; and every tongue that shall rise against thee in judgment thou shalt condemn. This is the heritage of the servants of the Lord, and their righteousness is of Me,***

saith the Lord." (*ref.* Isaiah 54:1-5, 17)

Having this biblical assurance, motivated me into believing the vision God had given me. And we acted on that vision by purchasing a building for ministry which appeared to be far beyond the current status of our ministry at that time.

Although the vision is for an appointed time there will come a time when you will be called upon to act upon your faith rather than upon your sight, because ***"faith without works is dead."*** Therefore, the reason why you can act with assurance is because ***"thy Maker is thine Husband!"*** And, as God was married to Israel, so is Christ espoused to His church. Therefore, the fruit of the relationship is not subject to the conditions of any natural or temporal circumstance. You must declare that you are never *barren!* No matter what area of lack you may be experiencing. How can you be barren when Your Maker is Your Husband and Your Husband is "The God of the whole earth?" This awesome God is omnipotent--all powerful! Just as the Spirit of God moved on the virgin womb of a young Jewish girl, named Mary, so does His divine anointing and omnipotent power bring life to the barren, death wombs of those espoused to Him in faith and ministry.

Know The Appointed Time and Move Without Fear

AS GOD PREPARED the way for our ministry to move, He challenged us to look beyond what we saw and possessed and move into a realm where His Word became our substance and our guarantee. We were challenged not to become paralyzed by circumstances, worries or fears. Although, in the past;

there have been times when our fears and apprehensions had been overwhelming but knowing it was the appointed time caused us to press forward without the paralysis of fear. Simply put, there are times when we are called to act and trust God for the results. The timing is important because God has arranged it--it's your appointed time! To have a time appointed is to have it *prepared* especially for you. Once God *arranges* your deliverance, your healing, or your prosperity, He *officially* sets your appointment and you are the only one that can be distracted from keeping it. Can't you see why the only device satan has is YOU. Satan will attempt many devices, but he MUST employ your cooperation to distract and make you miss your divine appointment with destiny. The arrangement is between you and God. Outside of you satan has no inclusion!

However, you can only know the time, if you are pregnant with purpose by your Husband and Maker. I am not suggesting that concerns over finances, resources and numbers of people never crossed my mind, but I found out that while I was permitted to be concerned about them, I was not allowed to be *full of care* (or careful) for them!

I remember praying one time about something I had prayed about several times before. In my new prayers, I began to ask God for a sign, even suggesting putting a fleece before Him. While I was mediating, I heard the voice of the Lord speak ever so clearly. He said to me, *"I've already given you a sign... and I've already told you what to do! If you fail to do what I have put in your heart, it's because of doubt and unbelief!"* God went on to assure me that it was "the time."

Your vision will die within you, if you don't move without fear to execute your portion. God does have a portion of the plan that He alone must complete, but He will only do *His* portion not yours. It is so sad that for the church, we live in a time where everyone is numbers-oriented. As leaders, if we aren't watchful, we too will be prone to count heads before making moves. This is a gross mistake, and in ministry it can be very costly. King David found out the dangers of census-taking when obedience and faith hangs in the balance. In ministry we all want growth, but health is more important. Moreover, the faith-challenging experiences which force one to go beyond appearances and resources not only serve to cause ultimate personal growth but it develops maximum spiritual growth as well.

Progressive movement is important to achievement. Adversities come to hinder, but we are the only ones who can stop our own progress. Some adversities are distractions, but distractions have no power to stop anything. When you allow yourself to worry excessively, you tend not to arrive at a decisive conclusion to your dilemmas. You tend not to trust your own decision-making abilities even when God is inspiring you. Yes, it *is* good to ponder decisions for wisdom. The Bible plainly exhorts us not to build without first counting the cost. God wants us to *prayerfully* count the cost and hear His voice so that when we do begin to move and other voices begin to speak we won't be distracted or confused. Trust the setting that God has prepared for you to move.

Praying or Stalling

GOD WILL ARRANGE the setting or stage. He will set the timing, but He will not make the move or act for you. Hence, the enemy of procrastination will come to render you helpless and inept. I will also caution you to be mindful of how often you declare that you are *"praying about it,"* when pondering a move for God. All of our decisions and actions should be the result of prayerful leading with time allowed for hearing from

God.

You could be stalling every time you claim to be *"praying on it"*, and what will eventually happen is that circumstance will ultimately make the decision for you. This is why it is so important to first, get a Word from the Lord, second, exercise faith in that Word, third, allow it to come alive in your spirit and, finally, act upon it. The stage is set! Don't miss your cue! The script is His, but the performance is yours. Don't sit backstage afraid to go on, worrying about the possibility of falling! ***"God has not given us the spirit of fear..."*** (*ref.* 2 Timothy 1:7) Step out on faith and perform all that is within you!

10

DISCERNING DISTRACTIONS

"...The places, which once hid us as a haven, are no longer fortresses but places which must be fled, if only for a season. When the time comes to flee, you mustn't allow even the offer of positions or titles to distract you."

PRESIDENT Franklin Delano Roosevelt once said in his first inaugural address, "...The only thing we have to fear is fear itself!" I'm sure when he first coined this phrase he didn't know the full spiritual ramifications of this statement. It's amazing how fearful many people are of their uncertain future. Many would rather hold on to their familiar past, or the mundane and mediocre rigor of the present, than risk a chance at a brighter future.

Fear is a master of disguises, changing its appearance with the expert skill of a special effects artist. Once you face your fears you can begin the arduous but satisfying process of unmasking them, thereby revealing their true worthlessness. It was this very process which led to this book. There were feelings of excessive preoccupation with issues, worries and concerns, which when fully examined were intricate, mentally-constructed masks for basic fear. It appeared on the surface that I wasn't moving because I was worried about this or that detail which appeared to have been related considerations. Actually, I feared the risk of failure and the impending shame which comes with it. The worry became a camouflaged agent for the fear to distract me and render me immobile, so I could not accomplish my dreams or achieve my goals, and greater still fulfill the will of God.

Have you ever experienced a situation where the moment you made up your mind to be all that the Lord desires you to be, you are suddenly acquainted or reacquainted with a task, a problem or even a familiar individual, which draws you away? They resurface, as it seems, from the bowels of hell as a demonic spirit on a mission though masked with an unassuming face, known or unknown. That is no coincidence! That is a distraction. Moreover, if you have managed to defeat satan's little distractions and move into a realm of obedience, you must be extremely watchful.

Satan is planning an unexpected attack designed to distract you so severely that it will become hard to get back on course. No one is ever exempt. The methods satan employs may change, his timing and tools may differ but his quest to distract remains unrelenting. The truth is he wants to take you to a place of no return: death! If you are going to ever reach the full potential, which lies within you, you must learn to recognize a distraction for what it is worth and defeat it.

Anything that draws your attention to an object or in a direction at the time you should be focused on something else, is a distraction. Distractions come in various forms and modes. There are distractions of the senses and of the mind. All distractions aren't bad. This is why we must qualify the diversion to determine what sort it is. Sometimes we need to be distracted from what we are focusing on because where we are is of little or no value. Sometimes the distraction comes because God knows we are not to continue in the vein we've been going. We must verify where we are or what we are doing to adequately qualify the distraction.

A Circumspection Journey

WHILE WALKING through the woods during a church picnic, I discovered the true understanding of walking circumspectly, which is a sure remedy for ungodly diversions and distractions. Not having been raised in the country, nor being what one would consider a great outdoorsman--the wild isn't one of my favorite places or most familiar arenas. Therefore, while trying to walk to the baseball field where most of the members were, I had to walk over tree stumps, twigs and logs. There were dead branches hanging, leaves and fallen vegetation all around. I heard unfamiliar sounds and even felt the combination of flying insects and leaves brush against my skin. My sight was dimmed by the foliage, which only permitted random rays of light to filter through to my dimly-lighted path. Albeit, I walked in a manner that caused me to remain focused, watchful, and without distraction. I had one aim in mind, to get to the open field where the rest of the people were. After reaching my destination, I heard a voice say within me, "Now you know what it means to walk circumspectly!"

What God was showing me was that the world in which we live is just as uncertain and potentially hazardous as the wiles of the thicket. To walk circumspectly is not necessarily to walk gingerly. We can make it through if we are watchful in all things and don't allow ourselves to become distracted or fearful by everything we see or hear. Consider what God said to Israel as He was establishing principles for them to live by in their place of promise.

> ***"And in all things that I have said unto you be circumspect: and make no mention of the name of other gods, neither let it be heard out thy mouth."*** (Exodus 23:13)

God wanted His people to know there would be other things all around them to serve as hindrances, attractive alternatives and false securities. They were in reality diabolical distractions. If you live and walk circumspectly you will live victoriously, godly and soberly in this present world. By walking circumspect, you will also know the difference between distractions of the enemy and God's attempts to attract your attention. These are times when the attention of the church has become so distracted that even the devil knows if he makes it sound good or look attractive, or even appear spiritual he can attempt to seduce the people of God with the intoxicating effects of distorted prosperity. Consequently, there are those who live in a state of distraction. It's as if the pursuit of so-called blessings have become the opium of the church, which has us drifting off into a slumber at a time when we should be as watchful as the five wise virgins. (*ref.* Saint Matthew 25:1-13) This is why Paul wrote,

> ***"...Awake thou that sleepest, and arise from the dead, and Christ shall give thee light. See then that ye walk circumspectly, not as fools, but as wise. Redeeming the time, because the days are evil. Wherefore be ye not unwise, but understanding what the will of the Lord is."*** (Ephesians 5:14-17)

What the enemy doesn't want you to know is that the anointing, goodwill and favor of God produces prosperity--

the wholesome wealth and godly wisdom necessary for great success and its retention. This is indeed a time of unprecedented wealth and riches for the child of God, but we must always understand that ***"The blessing of the Lord... maketh rich and He addeth no sorrow with it."*** (*ref.* Proverbs 10:22) Don't allow the distractions of the enemy in an attempt to be prosperous, rob you of your divine inheritance in the areas of prosperity and wealth. Remember, ***"Wealth [not earned] but won in haste, or unjustly, or from the production of things for vain or detrimental use, [such riches] will dwindle away; but he who gathers little by little will increase them."*** (*ref.* Proverbs 13:11 AMP) ***"Blessed is the man that feareth the Lord, that delighteth greatly in His commandments. Wealth and riches shall be in his house: and his righteousness endureth forever."*** (*ref.* Psalm 112:3)

God's will can only be made clear, if we are watchful and keenly sensitive to the times, utilizing His eternal Word as a lantern to lighten our paths and His face as the star which shines over our destination. Remember, He guides His people with His eyes not with His hands. We, as the people of God, have become so consumed with seeking the provisional hand of God; we no longer seek His face. Remember, It is in the face of God that we behold His likeness, and we see the hope of His calling for us, and that we grow into the image of His dear Son.

God's Attractions and Diversions

CLEARLY AN EXAMPLE of how God uses distractions can be seen in the story of the burning bush. God diverted Moses' attention with a burning bush to announce to him a new assignment. However, before He did, He had to upset Moses' world. Moses was raised in Egypt, but Egypt was only designed to preserve and sustain Moses until God could use him in another time and in another place. When he became of age for God to bring him into his destiny, God had to send trouble to Moses, thus causing Moses to flee. Moses' destiny was to be a deliverer. The place where Moses had been reared and where he was cultivated had turned into a place of obscurity. The same place, which once was a place of security had become a place of captivity. As a Hebrew, he was captive in his spirit though physically liberated. God knows you can't be a deliverer if you're captive. Although the murder of the Egyptians was wrong and it caused Moses major troubles, it was also the means by which God removed Moses from a captive place of worldly comfort and seducing luxury to a place where He could show Moses His will. God did this by circumstantially diverting his attention.

Just as God used the tragic events of a murder and the fugitive activity of a runaway, likewise God continues to manifest His divine providence in the lives of His chosen vessels, who also find themselves in tumultuous circumstances. If the truth be told, many of us came to a place of surrender through the pains of suffering and trouble. For most of us trouble got our attention and made us look to God in prayer! Like the prodigal son, trouble made us come to ourselves!

Grace That's Greater Than Our Sins

THE AWESOMENESS OF GOD'S GRACE is that it supercedes our errors and shame. That's what makes it grace coupled with the fact that it is freely given by God and without merit. It is even God's favor that drives us, with the force of His splendor and sovereign character, away from the mundane and familiar to a desert place of solitude, solace, and surrender. He skillfully does this while working all things together for our good, simply to attract our attention so that we might accept our predestined assignment. For it was in the desert place where Moses saw the burning bush which would not be consumed. Remember, it's not uncommon for distractions to come. Just as it was not uncommon for a bush to burn in the wilderness-desert. It was hot! Dried, bleached-parched bushes often caught fire in the savage heat of the burning desert. However, God usually takes the common and uses it in an uncommon manner to get our attention. That seems to be His way since He uses the same means to perform in our lives.

Those who are mightily used of God are not to be placed on some grand pedestal as though they are some featured attraction. We are all just burning bushes designed to attract other individuals who have lost their way and may go in the wrong direction. This is how we know God is seeking our attention. He often uses dead, discarded things to manifest His awesome glory, purpose, and power. He quickens us and set us on fire. But we don't become an attraction for God until we first have been drawn away into that place of solitude. Although Moses was attracted by the burning bush initially, his encounter with God caused him to subsequently become a burning bush. He was consumed with the fire of purpose, never to be the same again.

We wonder why certain types of troubles come which cause us to leave places of familiar surroundings, family and friends. The truth is, God wants to bring us to that spiritual place for which we were created. He knows very well that where we are is a comfortable and familiar place and though we may desire some growth and change, we really don't want our familiar world upset! Even if it's not very comfortable, it is at least familiar. And by human nature we tend to grow comfortable with that which we know. Even if we never leave some places physically we must leave spiritually. Once God has gotten us away, He even allows the well-known to become so distorted that we can't go back even if we wanted to. The haven that once hid us is no longer a place of fortification but a place, which must be fled, if only for a season. When the time comes to flee, you mustn't allow even the offer of positions or titles to distract you.

It is this aspect of destiny which is so bittersweet. Consequently, many people resort back to defeating behaviors because they are at least familiar. Thank God, He has something better in mind for us! When destiny is upon us He refuses to let us stay where we don't belong, even using the blast of affliction to release us like miners releasing precious resources. It saddens me to know that even when God allows some people to taste a small bit of the blessings He desires to give them, they seem to sabotage their blessing for fear of the unknown. They seem to stay in captivity or return to it out of fear.

Familiar Failure and Unknown Success

BEFORE GOING INTO full-time ministry, I worked in public service for the State as a rehabilitation specialist. In that job I would assist people with disabilities in obtaining the necessary training for job readiness and employment. While working in that job I discovered several things. First, I learned that the streets are filled with some of the most brilliant and capable people anywhere. The second discovery had to do with persons who battle with substance abuse. More often than not many of the people I helped got extremely close to finishing school or some sort of training. Those placed on jobs came close to completing their probationary periods, and without any notice they suddenly did something absolutely ridiculous to lose their job. Others simply disappeared, thus causing them to lose the opportunity they worked so hard to achieve.

If by chance, I was able to see them again or they came back at a later date for services, I would ask them "Why did you mess up your opportunity?" They would often reply, "I was scared!" When asked, what they were afraid of..., they wouldn't say, "failure," but after talking with them they saw it wasn't really failure that frightened them after all. They were most comfortable and familiar with failure. They really feared success. The reason for the sabotage was fear of the unknown. As it is in the natural, so it is in the spiritual! There are many saboteur-believers with the propensity toward the undermining the work of the Holy Spirit and sabotaging their spiritual destinies.

It's Just A Distraction

WHEN IT IS TIME to move to the place where we belong, the devil will offer us counterfeit blessings to distract us from our goal. Even in ministry, there are individuals who would rather surrender to offers of titles or positions, which may not be ordained of God, than to trust God with the course of their future. Often they simply can't conceive how God could be in anything that they are not actually controlling.

Therefore, we must be careful when attributing something to God simply because it's working according to our plans. There must be a litmus test to see if the element(s) are being sent into our lives to divert our attention or not. In order to test a distraction you must know your assignment, or at least, what the will of the Lord is for you. Then you must ask yourself if you are pursuing the course God would have for you. Where is your focus? You must know if you are being called back to your place or if you are being drawn away. If you discover that a job, position or title, money or fame is drawing you away from what you know God has called you to, don't try to make it be God's will when you know it's not. You must see it for what it is and flee as fast as you can.

In Moses' case God had to take him away to bring him back to the place where he would be used as a deliver. This is why God attracted Moses' attention by telling him to remove his shoes. The removal of his shoes did not only indicate his reverence for sacred ground but it served as a divine line of demarcation. This was the dividing place where Moses' path and course would forever change—between where he had been and where he was going.

Contemplation Which Leads to Disaster

AS WHAT WE SEE or hear can distract us, we can also be distracted by what we think. Nothing can be more distracting than anxiety. When we are anxious, we tend to be more easily distracted in our minds and emotions. We have thoughts and imaginations which can be limitless in its form. Once you start worrying about something, it can take on any form you imagine. A problem, no matter how small, can become as big as you can picture it.

With Moses we saw an example of a godly distraction, now let's look at a demonic one. It was only for a brief moment that Adam and Eve allowed themselves to be distracted both by what they saw and heard through anxiety. They had heard the voice of God, listened to the rationale of the serpent, saw the pleasantness of the fruit, and felt the emotional sensation stimulated by the imagination of their minds. The thoughts of possibilities and consequences, truth and lies, caused them to worry if they were not possibly missing out on something. They considered the question, "Is God keeping something from us?"

The Bible doesn't indicate how immediate it was between the time satan spoke to Eve and she convinced Adam to eat, but I believe they *worried* about the tree before a decision of disobedience was made. They imagined what it would be like to eat and savor the succulent taste of the unknown. They dissolved their worries with the rationale of saying, "How bad could the consequences be?" It was the thoughts they pondered which lead to their sin of disobedience. (*ref.* Genesis 3:1-7)

Satan too wants us to taste the forbidden fruit produced from the pride of life, the lust of the eye and the lust of the flesh. Like Adam and Eve, contemplation of thought will also say to us, "Do it. How bad could the consequences be?" From the voices of those who yet speak from the grave to those of us alive by His mercy and honest enough to admit it, we can declare, "It simply is not worth it!" Contemplation over things for which you already have an answer will only lead to disaster. What good is it to have the Holy Ghost and then not listen to His voice when He speaks, or follow His lead as He directs? Why ponder anything that God has clearly said to do or not to do! Even if it appears as though time is passing you by, ultimately, disobedience is too big of a price to pay.

Here's another example. Saul, the first king of Israel, in all his insecurities couldn't be obedient to God, because he worried about pleasing people rather than satisfying God. We must come to see that the preoccupation with thoughts, which are hindrances to our obedience are lethal distractions which must be avoided at all cost. Saul worried about provisions and personal security, in other words, worldly prosperity. He thought by keeping God's absolute plan it would cause him to miss out on something. This type of thinking or mind-set is of the devil, stemming from the same lie satan told

Adam and Eve. Look at what Saul did when God told him to kill everything of the Amalekites. Samuel told Saul, "God said to utterly destroy the enemy. Do not save anything alive." Saul destroyed everything except the king (Agag), and the best of of the spoil which he kept for himself. When Samuel heard the sound of the hidden sheep, he confronted Saul. Saul explained that he saved the best of the spoil to offer sacrifices. (*ref.* 1 Samuel 15)

Even today, men and women continue to disobey God by satisfying their self-centered motives, and think they can appease God by worshipping or offering Him their ill-gained sacrifices. But the greatest sacrifice we can offer God is our absolute obedience. Although Saul sought to blame it on the people, he was reproved by being told ***"to obey is better than sacrifice... For rebellion is as the sin of witchcraft, and stubbornness is as iniquity and idolatry."*** (*ref.* I Samuel 15:21-23) Have you been challenged by God not to touch something or, even greater, to destroy something which appeared to be worth holding on to? When we look at these and other examples we understand the value of true security. As we come face to face with the obedience of God we must let go of all false security and self-satisfaction trusting God's infinite wisdom.

There are times when we are just like Saul, Adam and Eve. We can't enjoy the blessings God has already given us, worrying about what we are missing. By obedience to God we are missing the hard ways of the transgressor. We are missing failure and misfortune. Most of all, we are missing life outside of His will and glory. We are missing the horrors which come from a desire to be in communion and fellowship with God. It's the horror of knowing your ways have so displeased Him that you're not sure if you will ever feel His anointing again. This is why David's 51st Psalm continues to be the pleading hymn of all that cherish God's grace and forgiveness:

"Create in me a clean heart, O God; and renew a right spirit within me. Cast me not away from Thy presence; and take not thy holy spirit from me." (vs. 10-11)

Single Servants Without Distractions

WORRY BRINGS DIVERS QUESTIONS to our minds which tug at us for self-satisfying action. It leads to impulsiveness, inspired by the confused notion that I must do something! This is not the lifestyle God intends for us to live. Not when He has provided for us means such as prayer and His Word by which we can clearly hear and know His voice. Once we have prayed and heard His word we are still ultimately left with the task of obediently waiting while trusting His wisdom.

Obedience must be practiced. Paul sets forth in I Corinthians 7:35, that distractions of the flesh come to affect your devotion to God. The AMP version reads,

> *"Now I say this for your own welfare and profit, not to put (a halter of) restraint upon you, but to promote what is seemly and in good order and to secure your undistracted and undivided devotion to the Lord."*

Paul used the subject of singleness and marriage to appropriately address where the believers' focus should be. His purpose for the discussion is stated in verse 32 where he clearly states he is addressing the matter, "...to have you free from all anxiety and distressing care." In other words, he deals with the appropriate priorities so that we would be free of distracting worries, which ultimately affect our relationship with God.

Paul concludes that if you are a single believer and not actively engaged in ministry, it is because you are distracted by something else. Single believers' attention should be focused on constructive things, toward the kingdom of God. Single people in the kingdom should occupy the greater portion of activity and responsibility for ministry in our churches. On the other hand, if you are married and you are so busy with ministry that your marriage is falling apart, you too are distracted! If we are going to handle distractions we must recognize the diversions for what they are, regardless of how attractive or noble they may appear. This is often how satan affects most people of destiny. Try every spirit by the Word to see what sort it is. Run the race set before you, for the King's business requires haste! By so doing, you will not only experience victory in your life but you will see His purpose fulfilled.

11

DON'T WORRY BE HAPPY

"Knowing the devastation which comes from something as simple as worry should create for us an alarm which will activate in itself in our minds whenever this menace appears."

IT WAS THE DECADE of the eighties and the climate of our society was mixed with subtle but invasive effects of Reaganomics. In what President Ronald Reagan called, "an era of renewal," we saw a resurgence of racial separatism with a new sophisticated appeal. Like it or not, for better or for worse, we also saw social welfare programs were severely threatened with the poor uncertain of their politically-influenced plight. Some called it the best of times, others said it was the worse of times. Yet, it took an accomplished musician, singer and composer, to surface with a light-hearted song, with an elementary-type melody and haunting familiarity. Its reggae sound and simple lyrics took the nation by storm. Bobby McFerrin reminded us of simple pleasures by simply saying, *"Don't Worry, Be Happy"* and the message was at least heard, landing him a Grammy Award for his composition.

It amazes me how sometimes the world can grab hold to a concept and seem to embrace it with such zeal, when all the while the principle is actually biblical. As trite as it may sound, worry can indeed rob us of our happiness, joy and peace. Moreover, the effects of the thief can be realized holistically. Far too many of us have witnessed the emotional effects which worry causes, manifesting itself through nervous and fearful apprehensions. Physical manifestations of worry are realized through pre-mature aging, hair loss, rapid heart rate and the like. The spiritual ramifications are only the tip of the iceberg resulting in an absence of peace, an inability to trust, inconsistency in commitment, and a lack of faith. The actions associated with this lack of faith, impassivity, and self-reliance will all assuredly lead to disobedience, which is sin. For all unrighteousness is sin. Knowing the devastation which comes from something as simple as worry should create for us an alarm which will activate itself in our minds whenever this menace appears.

Maintain Right Motives

YOU CANNOT ALLOW yourself to worry about past errors or areas of deficiency and thus become paralyzed and ineffective. You cannot worry about the results of decisions which must be made even when the outcome is uncertain. One must always do the right thing for the right reason, making sure your motives are pure. Once this is done, you must simply trust God for the results. If you approach every task or situation hoping to gain one hundred percent approval, you will only set yourself up for more anxiety and failure in life. Trying to please everyone will cause you to fail before you start. This is a sure way of displeasing God and robbing yourself of the happiness He has destined for all who would walk in His will! If you are not watchful, walking circumspectly, people will distract your focus and cause you to miss your appointed season.

There may still be those who ask, "But who is truly happy?" Well, according to Psalm 128:1-2, ***"everyone that feareth the Lord, and walketh in His ways"*** is sincerely happy. It is clear to see that true happiness does not come from pursuing happiness but from knowing God. David said, ***"... Happy is that people whose God is the Lord."*** (*ref.* Psalm 144:15) And, Psalm 146:5 declares, ***"Happy is he that hath the God of Jacob for his help."*** Therefore, it seems to me if anyone should be singing to himself, *"Don't Worry Be Happy,"* it should be the child of God! Don't be robbed of your song!

CONCLUSION

We must denounce any thought or imagination, which would exalt itself above the knowledge of God. Even when we have heard God's voice, we must move immediately in obedience, dispelling thoughts of worry as they come to distract. If we can bring our thoughts subject to God, then it won't be difficult for our wills and our actions to follow suit. Remember the Bible declares that ***"if you are willing and obedient, you shall eat the good of the land."*** (*ref.* Isaiah 1: 19) Many people are willing to do God's will, but they are not obedient because they are continuing to think thoughts of contemplation that consume time and/or lead to wrong actions. Once you capture the enemy of worry and bring it subject to God, you will continue to experience daily victory fulfilling the law of God.

If the Davidic purpose of Psalm 51 is ever achieved by this

book, then our suffering and pain would not have been in vain. If after all, transgressors are still taught the ways of God and sinners are ultimately converted, there is no need for us to worry about these light afflictions, which all will assuredly work for us a more exceeding weight of glory.

"AH, FILL THE CUP: —WHAT BOOTS IT TO REPEAT.
HOW TIME IS SLIPPING UNDERNEATH OUR FEET:
UNBORN TO-MORROW, AND DEAD YESTERDAY,
WHY FRET ABOUT THEM IF TO-DAY BE SWEET!"[4]

Edward Fitzgerald
1809-1883

About the Author

BISHOP Carl H. Montgomery, is a powerful preacher and teacher. He has through the written word now launched into a new arena with this life-changing book. He, along with his wife, Sheila, pastor the Greater Grace Church of Jesus Christ in Baltimore, Maryland. They are the proud parents of one daughter, Yeve Gennele. He holds a Bachelor of Theology from Loyola College, a Masters of Education degree in Counseling from Coppin State College and he is currently pursuing doctorate degree.

The bishop is the founder of Grace of God Ministries, Inc. and is a Certified Professional Counselor (CPC). He is the Assistant Presiding Bishop of The United Pentecostal Churches of Christ (UPCC), presiding over the Second Episcopal Diocese. He is also the UPCC as the Endorser of Chaplains for the U.S. Armed Forces.

MORE BOOKS...

If you have enjoyed this book be sure to let us know; and also look for these titles soon to be released by the author:

"THE CHURCHMAN: A Study in Churchmanship"
ISBN 0-9678976-1-0
SUMMER 2000

"THE CHURCHMAN"
The Workbook and Study Guide
ISBN 0-9678976-2-9
FALL 2000

"GET RID OF THE STUFF"
ISBN 0-9678976-3-7
SPRING 2001

PLEASE CONTACT US AT

GRACE OF GOD MINISTRIES, INC.

To receive the ministry's free newsletter,
The OLIVE BRANCH

or

- To invite the ministry of
Pastor(s)
Carl and Sheila Montgomery

REFERENCES

1 *Counseling and Values,* Vol. 44, No. 1, The Official Journal of the Association of Spiritual Ethical and Religious Values in Counseling, October, 1999, page 55.

2 Ct. *Ibid.,* page 55.

3 Ct. *Ibid.,* page 56.

4 The Oxford University Press, 2nd ed., Dictionary of Quotations, New York: Crescent Books, 1985.

5 Ogilvie, Lloyd J., gen. ed. The Communicator's Commentary Series, *Mastering The New Testament: A Book-By-Book Commentary By Today's Great Bible Teachers, Vol. 8:* Dunnam, Maxie D, *Galatians, Ephesians, Philippians, Colossians, & Philemon;* Dallas: Word, Inc., 1982.

OTHER WORKS CONSULTED

Zodhiates, Spiros, ed., *The Complete Word Study New Testament,* Iowa: World Bible Publishers, Inc., 1991.

CONTACT:

GRACE OF GOD MINISTRIES, INC.
Post Office Box 41350
Baltimore, Maryland 21203-6350

Voice: (410) 547-1118; Fax: (410) 547-1818
E-mail: bishiopchm@aol.com